3/88

Arts and Crafts
of the
Cherokee

Arts and Crafts of the Cherokee

RODNEY L. LEFTWICH

*Professor and Head of the Department of
Industrial Education and Technology*
Western Carolina University
Cullowhee, North Carolina
(Retired)

Cherokee Publications
P.O. Box 256
Cherokee, NC 28719

ACKNOWLEDGEMENTS

The author gratefully acknowledges the help and co-operation received from the following for their ideas, information and photographs contributed to this book:

Cherokee Historical Association

United States Department of the Interior,
Indian Arts and Crafts Board

Qualla Arts and Crafts Mutual, Inc.

Cherokee Indian Schools

Museum of the Cherokee Indian

The many Cherokee Craftsmen who supplied information and furnished craft items for photographs.

DEDICATION

To my wife, Janie; and
my children, Linda, Rodney,
Brent and Phil.

TABLE OF CONTENTS

ILLUSTRATIONS

All photographs were made by the author except where courtesy credit is shown.

Cover design by Rodney H. Leftwich, son of the author.

XII

INTRODUCTION

Traditional Cherokee arts and crafts in basketry, pottery, woodcarving, weaving, beadwork and stone crafts are being perpetuated today by the Eastern Band of Cherokees. This remnant of their once powerful nation now numbers about six thousand seven hundred and forty and lives on a fifty-seven thousand-acre reservation, the largest organized Indian reservation east of Wisconsin. This tract of land is located in the highlands of Western North Carolina in the heart of the original Cherokee Nation, where the country is as beautiful as the world affords. These Indians are the direct descendents of those Cherokee who, in 1838, hid out in the Great Smokies to avoid being moved from the land of their birth when the Federal Government attempted to force all Cherokee to move to reservations in Oklahoma. They are considered to be the most progressive and most self-sustaining of all the Indian tribes in the United States today. They have learned many things from the white man, but mass production has never been accepted in the construction of their arts and crafts. Each piece is truly handmade.

The village of Cherokee is unique in that it is without a single Cherokee home. It is a village of shops where Cherokee crafts are sold either by the Indians themselves or by white traders who have leased the establishments. From the sale of their crafts many Cherokee obtain a major portion of their income.

Practically all of the genuine Cherokee crafts found in their shops are constructed in their homes. These Cherokee homes are located back in the hills along the old trails that have been used for hundreds of years and wind back into every creek and hollow. Skill and knowledge in craftsmanship have been practiced and handed down from mother to daughter and father to son for generations.

For a long time there were only a few small shops selling handicrafts on the reservation. It was a familiar scene to see Indians traveling along the road from farm to farm and town to town with their backs piled high with an assortment of colorful baskets. Mrs. Lottie Stamper, who was born January 4, 1907 in the Soco section of the reservation, taught basketry at the Cherokee School for many years. In an interview with the writer, Mrs. Stamper told how as a child she watched her mother prepare and work white oak splints into baskets, and at the age of ten she started making them herself. She said that before good roads attracted visitors to the reservation, she walked long distances with her mother to Waynesville and Junaluska (twenty-five miles) to sell their baskets. They sold feed and garden baskets at the farms along the way and souvenir baskets to visitors attending the Summer Assembly at Lake Junaluska. With the money they received for their baskets they went into town and purchased shoes, clothing, and other items. Mrs. Stamper said that she had paid for every pair of shoes she has ever worn with money derived from the sale of her baskets. The Cherokees did not always receive cash for their baskets, but often traded them for cured meat, tobacco, or clothes.

After the Great Smoky Mountains became a National Park and good roads were built over the surrounding mountains, making it possible for visitors to reach Cherokee easily, it was no longer necessary for the Cherokee to leave the reservation to sell his wares. As the demand for handicrafts increased on the reservation, the Indian Service Personnel realized there were definite economic advantages to be gained for the Cherokee from the sale of his handicrafts and, therefore, encouraged the making of more and better craft work.

The National Park Service reports that the Great Smoky Mountain National Park, adjoining the Cherokee Reservation, has more visitors each year than any other National Park. Generally, tourists travel during the summer months; and in the winter many of the craft shops are closed, with only a few

Display and sales of genuine Cherokee crafts are handled in this attractive native stone building operated by Qualla Arts and Crafts Mutual, Inc. The building is located in Cherokee, North Carolina near the entrance to The Mountainside Theatre. Courtesy Indian Arts and Crafts Board.

traders buying articles in the off season. Though the Cherokee made most of their craft work during the winter, they often had to hold it until spring or sell it at low prices.

To relieve this situation about sixty Cherokee craftsmen, with the aid of the Indian Service Personnel, formed the Qualla Cooperative in the summer of 1946. This organization, whose membership has now grown to well over two hundred, is limited to Cherokee Craftsmen who make craft work of high quality. The purposes of the cooperative are "to provide a year-round market for Cherokee handicrafts, to promote high standards of workmanship and design, to help craftsmen solve their problems, and to secure better prices for craft work." Members may sell their work where they choose, but many of them market it entirely through the cooperative. The buying center and retail sales outlet for the cooperative is located in an attractive native stone building on the Reservation near the entrance to the Mountainside Theater, home of the Cherokee drama "Unto These Hills."

Since 1963 the cooperative, with the assistance and guidance of the Indian Arts and Crafts Board, has sponsored numerous demonstration workshops for the purpose of improving technologies in existing skills and introducing new techniques and media to Cherokee craftsmen.

The problem of the Cherokee today is not how to sell his products, but how to increase production to meet the demand of visitors to the Reservation and still maintain the high quality of hand work for which he is known.

The visitor to Cherokee should be cautious to make sure he is purchasing genuine Cherokee crafts. Because of the great influx of tourists, a considerable amount of factory-made and imported merchandise has been shipped in.

In order to help protect the public from this type of goods, the Federal Trade Commission issued a news release in 1968 stating that the term "Indian made" or the unqualified terms "Indian," "American Indian" and terms of similar import, should not be used to describe or designate products which have not been handmade or handcrafted by Indians resident within the United States. (Nothing in this statement should be taken to restrict the use of accurate descriptions of products manufactured in the Republic of India.)

The news release further states that: "Should investigation disclose that there is a violation of law, the Commission will move within the scope of its jurisdiction and remedial powers to correct the illegality."

The great variety and high quality of the hand crafts on display at the Cherokee Indian Fair in the fall of each year bear testimony to the skill and training of the present day Cherokee. All entries in the fair must have been made in the year since the last fair. They are judged on originality, beauty, design, usefulness and excellence of workmanship. First, second and third prizes are awarded for each listing. These awards are furnished by the Cherokee Historical Association. A recent Cherokee Indian Fair program listed thirty-nine categories of arts and crafts premiums.

Oconaluftee Indian Village, conceived by the Cherokee Historical Association, is a re-creation of a Cherokee Indian village of 1750. It is located on the Reservation near the Mountainside Theater. Here visitors see Cherokee men and women carry on an ancient way of life, practicing the centuries-old arts of basket-weaving, finger-weaving, pottery, and weapon-making. Cherokee craftsmen with primitive axes are engaged in hollowing dug-out canoes from poplar trees that were saplings 200 years ago. Others are feathering arrows and blowgun darts, fashioning bow and arrows, and making blow-guns. It is a "living museum" where authentic arts and crafts of the eighteenth century are demonstrated.

The Cherokee Indians are in some respects the most remarkable natives of the United States. Their tenacity and recuperative powers as a tribe have scarcely a parallel in the native history of our country. Their work in the arts has been outstanding in spite of the fact that their towns were repeatedly destroyed by war parties in early times, forcing them to flee to the mountains, and in spite of the fact that in 1838 the largest part of their nation was forced to leave their beautiful mountain country and move west of the Mississippi.

HISTORICAL BACKGROUND

The Cherokee have contributed much to our knowledge of Indian art from prehistoric times to the present day. They were the mountaineers of the South, holding at the time of their first contact with the white man the entire Allegheny region, which included the southern tip of what is now West Virginia, the eastern edge of Kentucky, the western portions of Virginia and North Carolina, northern South Carolina, northern Georgia and Alabama, and nearly a third of Tennessee.

The Cherokee called themselves "Aniyunwiya," which means "Principal People" in their language. This can be justified, as they were the largest single tribe in the Southeast and one of the largest tribes north of Mexico. They are included in the group of tribes classified as the Woodland Indians.

Archaeology has been carried on much longer in the East than anywhere else in the country, and a vast number of facts have been gathered. There is much evidence from archaeology that the Cherokee were long-time inhabitants of the Southeast. From the mounds, shell middens, stone graves, and village sites of the Cherokee area, an enormous mass of specimens has been taken in an extraordinary range of shapes, sizes, and media.

Although there have been differences of opinion concerning the origin of the thousands of mounds of the Eastern area, sufficient evidence has been found and presented to conclude with reasonable certainty that the Cherokee were Mound Builders. Major J. W. Powell, for many years head of the Bureau of American Ethnology, has this to say: "The manufactured articles taken from the mounds are in no wise different from those found on the surface. In fact they prove

conclusively that the Mound Builders were the Indians themselves or their ancestors." Further evidence is presented in
the fact that certain mounds were known to have been built
after the coming of Europeans because of the presence in or
under them of iron, glass, and other things of European
manufacture. Althought the Cherokee, a detached southern
element of Iroquois stock, were probably Mound Builders,
the war-like Iroquois proper to the north show little evidence
of the trait. Mounds are found at nearly all the large Cherokee settlements.

The Cherokee, as did many other tribes, often buried objects of use or value with their dead. It is to this mortuary
usage that we owe the preservation of so many entire examples of aboriginal art. Valuable knowledge has also been
obtained from the countless thousands of potsherds which
the archaeologists have carefully examined and classified.

The recorded history of the Cherokee begins with the
year 1540 when the first entry into their country was made by
De Soto advancing up the Savannah on his fruitless quest
for gold in May of that year. The earliest Spanish adventurers
failed to penetrate so far into the interior.

Information recorded by the journalists of De Soto indicates that the Cherokee were well advanced in the arts at
the time of this first contact. The expedition was received in
friendly fashion and was often met by the Indians bearing gift
baskets of berries. Carrying baskets were also given De
Soto's men along with food of various sorts. The fact that the
chief and principal men of the tribes dressed in fine robes of
skins is an indication of their skill in tanning. A dressed buffalo skin given the expedition is described as "An ox hide as
thin as a calf's skin, and the hair like the soft wool between
the coarse and fine wool of sheep." The Gentleman of Elvas,
one of the journalists of De Soto's campaign, declared that
the vessels of pottery used by the natives equalled standard
Spanish ware and that some were used to store walnut oil
and honey. De Soto's expedition spent a month in the mountain region, but left without finding gold although there were
reports and evidence of mining in the area.

Traders were the first to make regular contact with the Cherokee. William Byrd is authority for the statement that Virginia traders were among them as early as about 1612. However, little was recorded during this period concerning their arts and crafts. Our best information on this subject came at a later time from the writings of John Lawson, James Adair, Lieutenant Henry Timberlake and William Bertram. Lawson's *History of North Carolina*, first published in London in 1709, tells of the author's travels and contacts with the Indians of this state. James Adair, after spending several years among the Cherokee and other southern tribes published Adair's *History of the American Indians* in London in 1775. Lieutenant Henry Timberlake, who made several trips to the Cherokee country and accompanied three Cherokee Indians to England in 1762, published his *Memoirs* in London in 1765. William Bertram traveled mostly in the Florida area, but made several trips to the Cherokee area. His book, *Bertram's Travels*, was first published in Philadelphia in 1791.

These early writers will be referred to later where they wrote about the specific crafts being described.

BASKETRY

Cherokee basketry has endured continuously from pre-historic times to the present day, and baskets are probably the best known craft product of the Eastern Band of Chero-kee today. Colorful baskets of white oak splints, split river cane and honeysuckle hang in front of every craft shop on the Reservation.

Several Cherokee families have in their possession large hand-woven baskets and shallow household baskets which have been handed down for more than one hundred and fifty years. These baskets, though quite worn and having an oc-casional replaced splint, still retain their shape; and their colors have been mellowed with the years.

EARLY BASKETRY

Archaeologists have found ample evidence in the mounds, caves and village sites of the Cherokee area to indicate that these Indians or their ancestors were skilled basket makers as far back as we are able to establish any record of their tribe. Basket materials have decayed except where they were found in dry caves or in contact with copper salts; but impressions on pottery and other clay surfaces have given us much information that indicates the Indian knew and used a variety of materials and weaves in their mat and basket work. Historical writers have mentioned, described and praised the baskets of the Cherokee from the time of De Soto's journey through the Cherokee country in 1540 to the present day.

Adair's general account is the best early statement we have on this subject: "They make the handsomest baskets I ever saw, considering their materials. They divide large swamp canes into long, thin, narrow splinters, which they dye

Cherokee basketmaker using split river cane. Oconaluftee Indian Village. Courtesy Cherokee Historical Association.

Cherokee woman fashioning a basket from white oak. Dark splints were dyed with black walnut root. Oconaluftee Indian Village. Courtesy Cherokee Historical Association.

Cherokee boy setting a fish trap made of river cane. Oconaluftee Indian Village. Courtesy Cherokee Historical Association.

of several colors, and manage the workmanship so well, that both the inside and outside are covered with a beautiful variety of pleasing figures; and, though for the space of two inches below the upper edge of each basket, it is worked into one, through the other parts they are worked asunder, as if they were two joined a-top by some strong cement. A large nest consists of eight or ten baskets, contained within each other. Their dimensions are different, but they usually make the outside basket about a foot deep, a foot and a half broad, and almost a yard long . . . Formerly, those baskets which the Cherokee made, were so highly esteemed even in South Carolina, the politest of our colonies, for domestic usefulness, beauty, and skillful variety, that a large nest of them cost upwards of a moidore."

Lawson, in describing the Indians of North Carolina, has this to say: "The Mats the Indian women make are of Rushes, and about five Foot high, and two Fathom long, and sewed double, that is, two together; whereby they become very commodious to lay under our Beds, or to sleep on in the Summer Season in the Daytime, and for our Slaves in the Night.

"A Great way up in the Country, both Baskets and Mats are made of the split Reeds, which are only the outward shining Part of the Cane. Of these I have seen Mats, Baskets, and Dressing-Boxes, very artificially done." The Cherokee priest would always stand on these cane mats when preparing medicine from herbs.

Baskets were made in a wide variety of shapes and sizes to serve many purposes. The pack basket, carrying basket, and storage basket aided the Cherokee in gathering and storing grain. Timberlake, in describing a feast he attended in a Cherokee town-house, says the food was "served up in small flat baskets made of split canes."

The Cherokee used baskets to catch fish, and are credited with teaching this skill to the white man. Adair reported: "The Indians have the art of catching fish in long crails, made with canes and hiccory splinters, tapering to a point. They lay these at a fall of water, where stones are placed in two sloping lines from each bank, till they meet together in the middle of the rapid stream, where the intangled fish are soon drowned. Above such a place, I have known them to fasten a wreath of long grape vines together, to reach across the river, with stones fastened at proper distances to rake the bottom; they will swim a mile with it whooping, and plunging all the way, driving the fish before them into their large cane pots."

An early recreational use for baskets is described by Stewart Culin in his publication, "Games of the North American Indian." "The Cherokee basket game is a 'parlor game.' It is used in the family circle to while away the long winter evenings. The dice are six beans cut in half, the one side showing the black husk and the other the white interior. Sometimes six pieces of wood or six grains of corn colored black on one side are used. The dice are shaken in a shallow basket (four inches deep by a foot square) and if one bean of a given color comes up it counts one, if none comes up it counts two for the player. From a pile of eighteen to twenty-four beans kept as counters, the corresponding number according to the score are put in front of the player. As soon as the counters are exhausted in the main pile, it becomes a contest between the players' piles and generally dwindles down into a contest between two. After the center pile is exhausted, two or three beans are taken from each player and this generally eliminates the weaker players. Most of the time two or three beans of a color come up and the player cries, 'konight!' (nothing), and passes the basket on to another player. If he scores, however, he gets another trial. Two partners may play against two others in this game and the women play against the men. An interesting phase of this game was the betting. The men generally bet a deer, squirrel, or rabbit and the women bet bread. If the men were beaten they had to hunt and prepare the wild game for a feast. If the women were beaten they had to prepare bread for a feast. This was generally chestnut or walnut bread."

Originally only two artificial colors were employed in the decoration of baskets: a black or deep brown obtained from boiled black walnut root, and a reddish color obtained from "puccon" root (Sanguinaria Canadensis). The rich yellow of natural cane furnished the foundation color of all cane baskets.

Frank G. Speck, in describing early Cherokee basketry, writes: "With the exception of the complex 'double weave', there is considerable uniformity of technique. In twilling, which is the prevailing weave, there are four fundamental variations showing some minor irregularities. The figure proportions in the designs themselves are determined by following out a certain mathematical scheme of over and under turns of the splints. This produces geometrical patterns within certain limits, such as diagonals, diamonds, horizontal or vertical zigzags, and combinations of these with a few minor variations.

"The baskets are rimmed with a thin oak hoop bound fast with hickory fibre—an infallible characteristic of the Cherokee. No other southern tribe except the Catawba seem to use it."

Cherokee men will help gather and prepare the materials for baskets, and a few of them are expert basket makers. By and large however, the women do the basketmaking. This is true of almost all basket-making tribes. It is a well-known rule in the early stages of progress that, with few exceptions, the user of an implement or utensil was the maker of it. Indian women used baskets to gather, store, and prepare food; so it was natural that they should be the makers. This tradition continues today.

MATERIALS FOR BASKETRY

In the manufacture of their baskets the Indians have ransacked the three kingdoms of nature — mineral, animal, and vegetable. The first two have been used chiefly for color and decoration, although some tribes have used various animal tissues and skins in their weaving. The basket maker, however, is chiefly dependent upon the vegetable kingdom. Nearly all parts of plants have been used by one tribe or another for this purpose — roots, stems, bark, leaves, fruits, seeds, and gums. For purposes intended in each area, it would seem as if the vegetable kingdom had been thoroughly explored and exhausted above ground and underground.

The principal materials used in basketry by the Cherokee are cane, white oak, honeysuckle, hickory bark, and various dyeing and decorating materials.

Cane *(Arundinaria tecta* and *Arundinaria macrosperma)* is also called river cane, since it grows along the banks of streams in the southern part of the United States. Cane is probably the oldest of the Southern tribe basket materials. Although a versatile material, it is very hard and quite difficult to work. Baskets made of it are called ihiy A^{n}talwidz a^n, "cane baskets".

Oak splits are obtained from white oak *(Quercus alba).* White oaks grow abudantly on the Reservation, and the only problem in procuring it is the selection of straight-grained young trees of the proper size. Baskets made of oak are called tall A^{n}taliwidy A^n, "oak baskets".

Sugar maple *(Acer Saccherum)* splints have been used by a few Cherokee basket makers in recent years. The splints have a shiny surface which is quite attractive, but they are rather brittle and more difficult to work.

Honeysuckle *(Lonicera Japonica) is* the most recently adapted basket material of the Cherokee. Since honeysuckle was introduced into this country from Japan less than one hundred years ago, it has become so thoroughly naturalized and has spread so rapidly that it is now one of our most common plants from the Atlantic to the Mississippi and from the Ohio River to the Gulf. The Cherokee were quick to see its possibilities as a basket material, and now they use the long, flexible stems in certain styles of their smaller baskets.

Hickory bark *(Hicoria ovata)* is made into a withe to bind the rim-hoops of their baskets. This use constitutes an earmark of Cherokee basketry because it is the only Southern tribe using it, with the possible exception of the Catawba.

Black walnut *(Juglans nigra)* and "puccon" *(Sanguinaria Canadonsis*, known to the Cherokee as bloodroot) were the only two materials originally employed to obtain artificial colors for decoration. Recently, as will be mentioned in more detail later, the Cherokee have employed a greater variety of native vegetable dyes and some commercial dyes.

HARVESTING MATERIALS

Though trade and barter have been common with the Indians as far back as we have any record, it is not to trade that the weaver looks for her basket-making materials. She has no store to which she can go and purchase cane, oak splints, honeysuckle or hickory bark ready-dyed and done up in bundles for her. She must find the materials in her own environment. This harvesting of materials embraces an intimate acquaintance with the places where just the right substances abound and knowledge of the times when each element is ripe or of the proper size. Some basket makers will gather their materials only at certain seasons when they say the sap is right; others claim that they can be gathered satisfactorily at any season. Selection for suitable grain and textures, methods of growing and harvesting, as well as the tools and apparatus used in gathering are all important to the basket maker.

The restricted locations which the Cherokee now occupy are somewhat too elevated and cool for cane to flourish in the immediate neighborhood. (Experiments have been conducted recently to test a new type of imported bamboo which will grow at the higher elevations. It was found that the bamboo was too brittle and would break at the joints while being worked.) Cane was secured for some time along the flats of the Tuckasegee River and transported on foot by back-loads to the present settlements of the Cherokee. As the supply of cane along the Tuckasegee became depleted, the Cherokee traveled over the mountain into South Carolina and returned with back-loads of cane. Today the Cherokee gather their cane where they can find it in Western North Carolina, South Carolina, from the banks of the Cumberland River in Kentucky and from the Hominy Valley Canebrakes in North Carolina. The Kentucky source of supply is the result of a treaty between the Cherokee Indians and people of Barbourville,

Kentucky, signed in 1950. This treaty provides free river cane from the banks of the Cumberland River for the Eastern Band of Cherokee Indians for use in making baskets and other handcrafts. It has been referred to as the first pact in American history that was solely of benefit to the Red Man. The agreement has no time limit. Under terms of the treaty, the Cherokee are given all the cane they want from the Kentucky canebrakes. In return the Cherokee promises friendship and a yearly pilgrimage to the Blue Grass State at which time they smoke the peace pipe with Kentuckians. The wording of the treaty follows:

> We the people of the Cherokee Nation and the people of Kentucky, in friendly council here assembled, do, make this solemn compact, to last until such time as the sun shall no longer shine, the birds no longer sing, and green things no longer grow on the earth.

> Article I.
> We, the people of the Cherokee Nation do agree to send to Barbourville, Kentucky, a delegation of one or more persons to visit our Kentucky friends.

> Article II.
> We, the people of Kentucky, do agree to repay the kindness of the Cherokee with gifts of cane for as many baskets as they can make.

> Witness our hands this 13th day of August,
> 1950 A.D. at Cherokee, N. C.

In 1969, the American Enka Corporation opened its canebrakes along Hominy Creek to the Cherokee Indians, whose ancient crafts of basketry and blowgun-making are threatened by a dwindling supply of native river cane.

In friendly council assembled on the stream's cane-lined banks, Enka officials and Oconaluftee leaders signed a solemn compact allowing the Indians to harvest the cane "as long as the green grass grows and the rivers flow."

In return, the Cherokee agreed to present annual tribute of one handcrafted river cane basket each spring to the holders of the green fields of Hominy Creek as a token of renewal of this treaty and of lasting friendship with their white neighbors of American Enka Corporation.

The Cherokee select large canes about the size of the thumb that are at least two years old. This cane is stronger than the year-old cane, it is not quite as green in color, and it may be identified by the extra quantity of foliage near the top of the plant. Cane may be worked into splints immediately after gathering, or it may be kept a reasonable length of time if it does not dry out too much.

The Cherokee basket maker has learned to identify the white oak tree by its flaky, light-colored bark. It grows abundantly on the Reservation as well as all areas of the Southeast. Trees of this species have been known to grow to a diameter of eight and one-half feet. Although white oak of any size and age may be worked into basket splints, the Cherokee generally select young saplings from three to ten inches in diameter. A log of this size can be transported by back from the forest to the cabin of the basket maker, and it is easier to split. It also produces the quantity of splints generally needed at one time.

Selection of the white oak sapling is of utmost importance. The tree must be straight and free from knots. White oaks growing in a thicket or close to other trees have a straighter grain and split more easily than trees growing alone. This is probably due to the protection from weather given by other trees in the thicket.

The part of the tree close to the roots is more difficult to split, so the basketmaker avoids this by cutting the tree twelve to fifteen inches above the ground. He then takes the straight trunk section up to the first limb. This is generally three and one-half to six feet in length. Some basket makers also make use of the straight lengths of trunk between limbs for shorter splints.

Only enough saplings for a few days' work are gathered at a time. Logs that have dried out are more difficult to split and the splints are not as white as those from fresh logs. The logs need no seasoning and are ready to be worked into splints as soon as they reach the basket maker's cabin.

Honeysuckle can be gathered and used at any time of the year, but it is at its best between September and April. It grows abundantly along roadsides, at the edge of forest, on banks, fences, and trees; but the selection of good honeysuckle requires careful searching. Nearly all the vines growing on trees, bushes, and fences are very crooked and full of branches. The good vines are literally out of sight and often overlooked by the person with an untrained eye.

The best honeysuckle of the small sizes will be found growing where it has no chance to climb. Where it has been growing in good soil for several years and has formed strong roots, it will cover the ground with a thick growth of vines running in all directions. These vines will twine very little and many of them grow straight and to great length without branches. Honeysuckle is a very fast-growing vine, often growing fifteen to twenty feet the first season, and making most of this growth in a short time. If the vine lives through the winter, it makes another growth the following spring and branches off from the tip of the previous year's growth. This may continue for several years, the diameter increasing each year. The first year's growth usually exceeds all the rest. While the vine is growing it is covered with leaves, and the bark at the tip is a purplish white, which changes to a light brown and becomes shiny and smooth. This new growth is not good during the first season, as it does not become tough and strong enough to use until winter. This growth will not have any leaves the following season and very few, if any, branches except at the tip. These vines at one or two years of age are suitable for weaving; and, as the new vines each year naturally climb to the top for light, those older vines become covered by the fresh foliage and must be searched for underneath. The color of the bark usually changes after the first year to a darker brown, gradually loses its smooth shiny surface, and sometimes becomes rough and gray in color. After several years' growth, these vines are apt to develop large knots which make them unfit for use.

Dead vines are of no use. These are easily detected by scratching the outer bark. The inner bark will show green if it is alive. All honeysuckle has a hole in the center, but the size of the hole varies greatly. If the hole exceeds one-half the diameter, the vine will be apt to flatten or split when used.

No tools are necessary in gathering honeysuckle. The vines are broken off near the roots by bending them sharply. They are then pulled free from the other vines, laid in long straight bundles and tied in several places. The bundles are then easily coiled and carried home.

PREPARING MATERIALS

In their rough state, many of the materials for basketry would be as unfit for use as quarry clay would be for the potter or crude ore for the metallurgist. The Cherokee, using the simpliest of tools, work the white oak logs, river cane, and wild honeysuckle into smooth, uniform materials for the warp and weft of their baskets.

The only tool needed for the preparation of cane is the jackknife. The worker cuts off and discards the small foliage-end of the cane. The large part of the cane is split lengthwise into four pieces. The basket maker then peels off the shiny outer surface of the cane. This is the part used in basketry (the coarse inner fiber of the cane is discarded). The cane splints are then trimmed along each edge to make them of uniform width. Scraping needs to be done on the inner surface only, because the shiny outer surface is part of the natural beauty of cane. These operations of splitting, peeling, trimming, and scraping produce strong flexible splints of uniform width and thickness.

To prepare oak splints, the logs are first split lengthwise by driving a wedge, hatchet, or splitting axe into the end of the log. A small log is split into four pieces. A larger log will produce six, eight or more pieces. From this point on the only tool the Cherokee uses to prepare his oak splints is a jackknife. Each log section is trimmed to remove the bark and splinters. The jackknife is then inserted into the end of the log section parallel to the annual rings and far enough from the edge to make a splint of the proper thickness. After starting the splint, the knife is laid aside and the splint is

River cane that has just been harvested for use in the making of baskets.

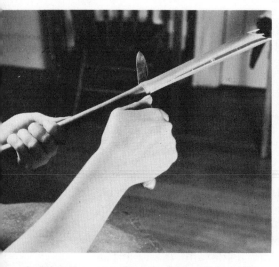

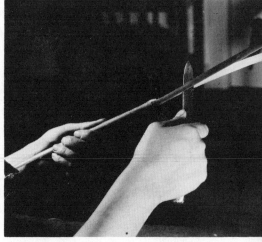

Splitting the cane. Cane is first split in half lengthwise. Each half is split again to make four pieces from each cane.

Peeling the cane. Each quartered piece of cane is split lengthwise to remove the shiny outer surface, which is the part used in basketry.

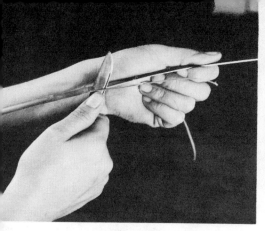

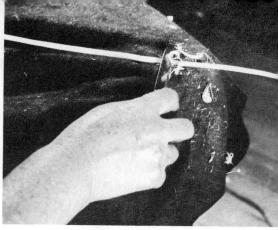

Trimming the cane to make the splints a uniform width.

Scraping the cane. This is done on the inner surface only, because the shiny outer surface is left to give a natural finish to the basket.

A bundle of prepared cane splints. These splints have been split, peeled, trimmed, and scraped.

Cherokee man pounding his splitting axe into the end of a small white oak log. This is the first step in the preparation of oak splints for basketry.

Oak splints are pulled apart with the hands after they have been started with a jackknife.

Honeysuckle that has just been gathered. It is rolled into a coil for convenience.

A bundle of honeysuckle with bark removed.

Mrs. Bradley coils hickory bark she has stripped from young saplings preparatory to placing it into a container to be boiled. The bark will be used to finish the tops of

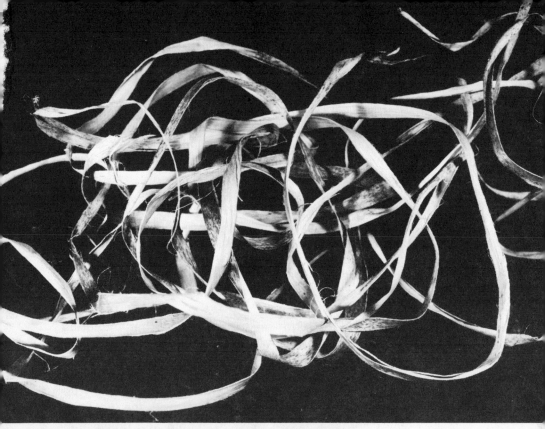

Hickory bark is used to bind down the rim-hoops of many Cherokee baskets.

Bark basket. Bark was probably used by Indians prior to oak and cane splints.

peeled off the full length of the piece by pulling it apart with the hands. Much care is needed in this operation in order to produce splints of uniform width and thickness. When a splint starts to thin out or split off, the pulling must be done with the opposite hand.

After the oak splints have been stripped from the log sections, they are next trimmed to an even width with the jackknife and then smoothed on upper and lower surfaces by scraping. In smoothing the splints the worker holds a knife, blade down, approximately even with his knees. The splint is drawn toward the worker beneath the knife. Some heavier splints are prepared from white oak for use as ribs, hoops, handles and the like.

Honeysuckle is quite easy to prepare. After gathering, the leaves and small branches are broken off. It is then coiled and placed in a deep pan, covered with water, and boiled until the bark begins to loosen. The bark can then be slipped off the vine by rubbing lengthwise with an old cloth. Any uneven joints, buds or knots are trimmed off with the jackknife.

Many Cherokee basket makers smooth and polish their honeysuckle vines by taking them to a stream where they use handfuls of sand to rub the vines.

If the honeysuckle vine is gathered at a time of year when the inner part of the vine is greenish instead of white, this greenish color may be removed by bleaching with any standard commercial bleach.

Hickory bark is prepared by peeling off long, narrow strips of bark from young hickory saplings. These are coiled, placed in a container, and boiled until the dark outer surface of the bark can be scraped off. This leaves a tough, tan-colored, flexible withe which the Cherokee use to bind down the rim-hoops of their baskets.

DYEING MATERIALS

The Cherokee depends largely on the natural colors of his basket materials for their charm and beauty. The rich yellow of the natural cane furnishes the foundation color of all the cane baskets, while the natural color of the oak splints and honeysuckle does the same for these baskets. The Cherokee, however, makes very few plain baskets so it is necessary to dye the materials that are worked into the design.

Vegetable dyes are considered superior to commercial dyes for basketmaking because they are softer, more harmonious and less effected by fading. Usually when they do fade they still bear a definite relation to their original color, and often become softer and more beautiful without losing their character; while a faded synthetic dye usually bears little resemblance to its original tone. The fact that colors obtained from natural sources do not usually deteriorate in quality, but sometimes improve, is a definite advantage in their use.

The sources of vegetable dyes may be the roots, barks, leaves, hulls, nuts, flowers, fruits, stems, seeds, or the complete plant. In many cases, the time of the year when these are gathered is important. This would be obviously true with flowers and fruits, but it is also true with certain roots and barks.

Cherokee basket makers' chief dye materials are black walnut, butternut, bloodroot and yellowroot. Brown is obtained from the bark or the root of the black walnut. The same parts of the butternut tree produce a strong black. The root of the bloodroot produces a red brown color. The bark of the twigs of the yellowroot gives a maize yellow. Some Cherokee use the common broom sedge to produce a color known as burnt orange that works beautifully in basketry. Although some basket makers on the Reservation have recently used a few commercial dyes, even these wisely restrict themselves to the original browns, blacks, and reds.

The large majority of native vegetable dyes are made by boiling the plant materials. For a dye pot an enameled kettle is generally used. In former days, a wash pot was used and dyeing was done out in the open. Sometimes the material to be dyed is boiled with the dye source and sometimes not. In every case, the dye must be boiling when the material is immersed. If the dye is too strong, it can be diluted; if it is found not strong enough, it can either be boiled down or more dye material added. During the dyeing process the material being dyed is turned over and over so that the color evenly reaches all the parts. A stick is used for turning the material.

The length of time required for the dyeing process varies from fifteen minutes to eight hours depending on the material being dyed, strength of dye and intensity of color desired. Cane is the hardest material and takes the longest time for the colors to pentrate. Oak splints and honeysuckle are softer and need be boiled only about half as long as cane to absorb an equal intensity of color. Dyeing is the final step in the preparation of basketry materials.

PROCESSES OF MANUFACTURE

After the basket materials are split, peeled, scraped, and dyed, they are ready for fabrication into baskets of varying size, shape, weave, and use. In all types of weave the working strands must be pliable. The Cherokee use the materials soon after preparation and while still filled with sap, or else they soak them in a bowl of water until they are flexible enough to work easily. They are kept damp or are redampened during the weaving process.

As one gazes on an Indian basket maker he will be amazed to find that she uses no models, drawings or patterns. Her patterns are in her soul, in her memory and her imagination, in the mountains, streams and forests, and in those tribal tales and myths that are a tradition with her tribe.

Various techniques are used by Indian basket-makers. A brief look at the over-all picture will help us to better visualize those types employed by the Cherokee.

There are two distinct types of techniques in basketry; namely, (1) handwoven basketry, which is built on a warp foundation, and (2) sewed or *coiled* basketry, which is built on a foundation or rods, splints, or straws.

Kinds of Woven Basketry:
   A. Checkerwork: The warp and the weft having the same width, thickness, and pliability.

B. Diagonal or twilled basketry: Two or more weft strands over two or more warp strands.

C. Wickerwork: Inflexible warp; slender, flexible weft.

D. Wrapped weft, or single weft wrapped: The weft strand is wrapped, or makes a bight about the warp at each decussation.

E. Twined or wattled basketry: Weft of two or more elements.

Kinds of Coiled Basketry:

A. Coiled work without foundations

B. Simple interlocking coils

C. Single-rod foundation

D. Two-rod foundation

E. Rod and welt foundation

F. Two-rod and splint foundation

G. Three-rod foundation

H. Splint foundation

I. Grass-coil foundation

J. Fuegian coiled basketry

All Cherokee baskets fall into the first three classifications under Woven Basketry. The only coiling technique used is in binding the rim-hoops of some of their baskets.

Checkerwork (also known as mat weave and plaiting) is used in most Cherokee oak-splint work. This occurs especially in the bottoms of the baskets and generally continues up the sides. In this ware, the warp and weft have the same thickness and pliability. It is impossible, therefore, in looking at the bottoms of these oak-splint baskets, to tell which is warp and which is weft. The warp and weft of a checker-bottom are usually turned up at right angles to form the warp of the sides and new splints are added for the weft.

Checkerwork baskets are started by placing a number of splints side by side to make the warp. Then weft splints are woven one at a time over and under the warp at right angles. As this continues a mat is formed and when the proper size for the bottom of the basket is reached all splints are turned up to form the warp of the sides.

This simple over-and-under weave makes a strong basket

Bottom of an oak splint and honeysuckle basket.

Weaving the sides of an oak splint and honeysuckle basket. Two weavers are used in this process and the basket maker is now ready to insert a new one.

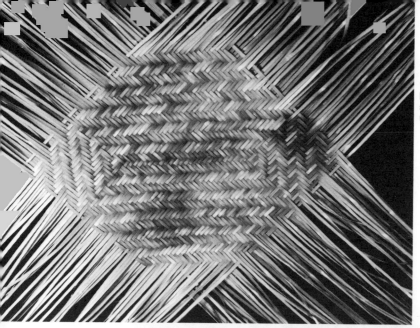

Bottom of a "double weave" basket ready for the sides to be turned up.

Partially completed "double weave" basket shows how sides are woven obliquely.

Crossed sticks or canes placed in the bottom of a basket during construction aid the basket maker to secure good form and contour. The sticks are removed when basket is completed.

Cane basket under construction shows how weft element is worked over-and-under the upright splints to create design.

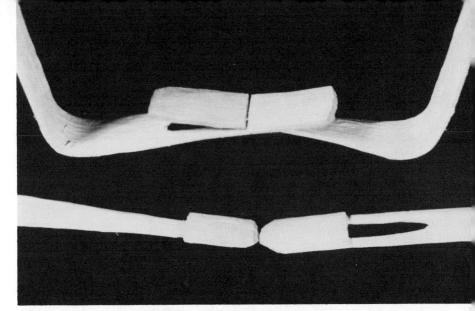

Cherokee basket handles of white oak. Lower handle shows how ends are carved. Upper handle has ends locked in place.

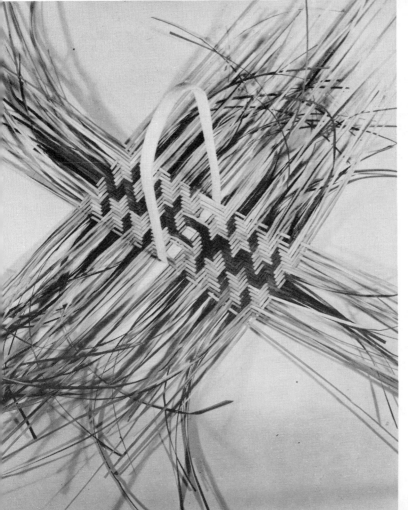

The handle of this cane market basket is woven in as the basket is made.

DENVER ART MUSEUM

1300 LOGAN STREET, DENVER, COLORADO

DEPARTMENT OF INDIAN ART

FREDERIC H. DOUGLAS, Curator

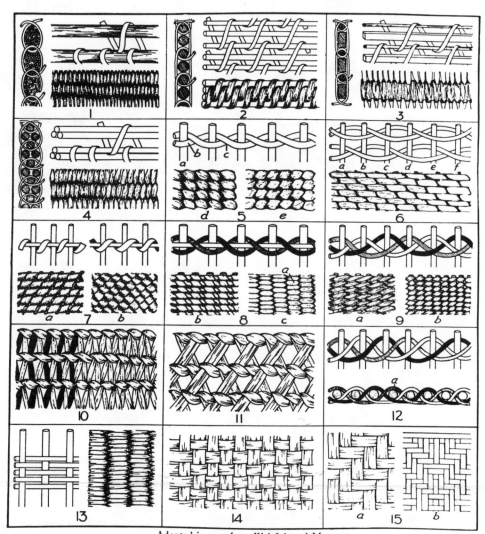

Adapted in part from Weltfish and Mason

BASKETRY CONSTRUCTION TECHNICS

LEAFLET 67

DECEMBER, 1935

2nd Printing, September, 1940

Basketry construction techniques. Reproduced from a Denver Art Museum leaflet. The Cherokee use only techniques 13 wickerwork, 14 checkerwork and 15 twilling in their baskets.

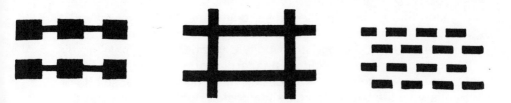

Early Cherokee basketry designs. Reproduced from **Decorative Art and Basketry of the Cherokee** by permission of the Milwaukee Public Museum.

and Cherokee basket makers have worked out an amazing variety of patterns and designs by varying the width and colors of splints used.

On certain of their baskets the checkerwork is left open to form the mesh of the sifters and winnowing baskets. The amount of opening is varied to fit the use of the basket; for example, a meal sifter would be woven with a finer mesh than a hominy basket. This checkerwork weave is used most often on the market baskets, waste baskets, rib baskets and fish baskets.

Twilling is the prevailing weave used in Cherokee cane basketry. The fundamental technique of twilledwork (diagonal basketry) is in passing each element of the weft over two or more warp elements, thus producing either diagonal or twilled, or , in the best examples, an endless variety of diaper patterns. The twilling technique dates back to prehistoric times in the Cherokee area.

In twilling there are four fundamental variations showing some minor irregularities, the following of which produce the different designs. The bottom of the basket is often begun with double splints in an over-two-under-two weave. When the walls are reached the weave is continued for from three to six courses, in what may be an over-two-under-two up to over-five-under-five technique, to the point where the design is begun. Here, too, the number of over and under turns ranges from over-three-under-three to over-five-under-five until the region near the rim is reached, when the pattern may change again. It will be seen, then, that the figure proportions in the designs themselves are determined by following a certain mathematical scheme of over and under turns of the splints. This produces geometrical patterns within certain limits, such as diagonals, diamonds, horizontal or vertical zigzags and combinations of these with a few minor variations. These designs are wholly dependent upon passing by or adding one or more standard (upright) splints in each course of the filling. The basket maker is more conscious of varying the weave to make the design right than counting the number of over and under turns.

The following tabulated figures, taken from an examination of the several collections mentioned, show the proportionate occurrences of the variations in the work of the Cherokee.

Cherokee Basketry collection	over-one-under-one	over-two-under-two	over-three-under-three	over-four-under-four	over-five-under-five	Total Specimens Examined
American Museum of Natural History, N. Y.	6	5	18	3		32
Museum of the American Indian, N. Y.	8	2	25	5	3	43
Milwaukee Public Museum	5	2	10	10	1	28
Cherokee Indian Reservation, N. C.	13	3	22	5		43
Specimens examined elsewhere	3		5	1		9
Totals	35	12	80	24	4	155

This table was taken in part from *Decorative Art* and *Basketry of the Cherokee* by Frank G. Speck. Those baskets studied on the Reservation and elsewhere were examined by the author.

The figures in this table represent the predominating technique in each basket, chiefly in the lower part of the sides and in the design area. Thus it appears that more than half of the specimens examined are woven in an over-three-under-three twill. Correlating the designs with these twill variations, we find the over-three-under-three more often employed in forming the diamond pattern, and the over-four-under-four more often in the chain pattern; usually, however, these two appear most frequently combined in the same baskets. Sometimes, to cite an ordinary case, we find a basket begun by the over-three-under-three process in the lower part and changed to the over-two-under-two near the rim.

At times, in both checkerwork and twilling, the warp and the weft may be worked up obliquely, instead of vertically and horizontally. The chief examples of this technique are to be found in the twilled "double weave" baskets of the Cherokee. These are by far the most complex of all their baskets. In the "double weave" the splints are laid diagonally on the bottom; that is, not at right angles to each other as in other forms. Then they are continued up the sides obliquely across the basket, the whole forming a diagonal twill. When the top of the basket is reached, the splints are bent over the rim and the oblique weaving is continued down the outside and under the bottom. During the first part of the weaving up to the rim, the flat, inner surfaces of the cane are turned out; as the splints are bent over the rim the flat surfaces are turned inside and the weaving continues in this manner. This exposes only the smooth, outer surfaces of the cane, thus the basket is completed in double facing, the inside and outside having only the glossy surface of the material showing. Even the patterns may vary inside and outside according to the number of under and over turns of the weave.

Wickerwork is probably the most common of all basket weaving techniques and is recognized as one of the most primitive forms of this industrial art. It is also known as the web weave, getting its name from the spider web appearance it has during weaving.

Cherokee use wickerwork in their honeysuckle baskets. This technique consists of a wide or thick inflexible warp and a slender flexible weft. The weaving is plain and differs from checkerwork only in the fact that one of the elements is rigid. The effect on the surface is a series of ridges.

Both mats and round baskets are made by this technique. If honeysuckle is used for the warp, the mat or basket is started by placing the required number of spokes at right angles to each other, then the weft strand is woven over and under this group for two full turns. The spokes are then spread into a radiating pattern. After spreading, the weaver goes over and under each spoke separately. Upon completion of one row, an odd spoke must be inserted or an extra weaver must be added, for proper web weaving can never be done with an even number of spokes and a single weaver. Cherokee basket makers generally use two weavers, allowing one to pass in front of the warp elements while the other passes behind them.

It is often necesssary as one weaver runs out to start a

new one. The end of the last weaver is left behind a spoke with about three-quarters of an inch to spare. This is crossed with an equal length of the new weaver and weaving proceeds. When the basket is completed and dry, the unnecessary ends are cut off.

Oak splints are often combined with honeysuckle in Cherokee sewing baskets and waste baskets. These baskets are started by placing the splints, which will serve as the warp, one by one across each other so that they will form a radiating fan pattern. The weavers of honeysuckle are inserted between two of the splints and held tightly with one hand while the other hand is used to work them in and out around the center. As the weaving continues, the spaces between the splints will increase in size. These spaces may be filled by adding a second group of splints placed so that they fall between those used to start the basket. When as many rounds as necessary are woven for the bottom, each spoke is bent up to form the foundation for the sides. The weaving of the sides continues in the same manner as the bottom. The tops of honeysuckle baskets are bound in place with a withe of hickory bark or white oak.

Some baskets, such as market baskets and shopping baskets, require handles. The Cherokee carve these from white oak or hickory. A type of handle that locks together is generally used to insure strength. After carving, the handle is soaked well and bent to the proper shape, tied securely in this shape and allowed to dry. Most handles are woven in as the basket is made rather than being added later.

The borders or rims of Cherokee baskets are finished in several ways. The purposes of the border are to strengthen the basket, improve its looks, and dispose of the upright warp elements. Checker or twilled weaving with the edges left open all around would be a flimsy affair. Coiled work lends a hand in putting a finish on woven work. The Cherokee generally use a binding withe of hickory bark or white oak for this coiling.

When the sides of an oak basket are ready to be finished, the last weft circuit is made with a thicker and wider weft than those used in the body of the basket. The warps that remain outside the last curcuit are cut halfway across from the right hand side, level with the top of the basket. The remaining half is shortened and sharpened and tucked down inside the basket under the wefts. The other warps are trimmed level with the top and then two rims are put in place. These rims, split from hickory or oak, are thicker than other elements of the basket and are rounded on their outer surfaces. The ends of each rim are tapered in order not to make it too bulky at the point where they cross. The basket is finished by binding these rims in place with a flexible withe of hickory bark or white oak.

In cane basketry the protruding ends of the upright standards are disposed of by winding them into the rim. This resembles closely the interlacing of a series of crossed warps. The rim hoops may then be bound in place to strengthen the top. Cherokee methods of finishing borders are similar to those used by other Southern tribes.

BASKETRY FORMS

Form in basketry is decided at the outset, not by the desire to create something artistic, but to produce a useful receptable. Although function is considered first, a sense of symmetry and other artistic qualities enter into the composition of all Cherokee baskets. The shapes of basketry have relation to the forms of solid geometry. The cube, the cone, the cylinder, and the sphere are the bases of all simple and complicated varieties. Most Cherokee baskets are cylindrical or rectangular in outline. In giving to basketry the forms just indicated, the Indian woman has always in mind the elements of the beautiful as well as of the useful. It is considered a reproach to violate the rules of bilateral symmetry or proportion in form. The manipulation of basket materials to produce baskets that are symmetrical and of pleasing contour is recognized as the most difficult task in basketry. Cherokee baskets are made in a wide variety of forms which may be classified as: flat forms, dish forms, bowl forms, jar forms, and miscellaneous forms.

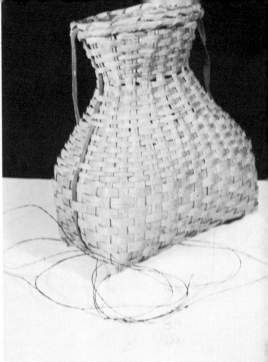

A Cherokee pack basket of white oak splints. Over one hundred years old. Note where new splints have been added. The top rim is bound with hickory bark.

Early Cherokee fish basket of oak splints. The basket was purposely made small so that the fisherman would not catch more fish at one time than he could use. A horsehair fishing line is shown with the basket. Museum of the Cherokee Indian, Cherokee, North Carolina.

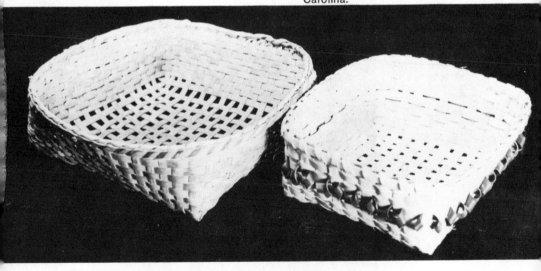

Hominy sifters. The one on the left is very old. The one on the right is a newer, fancier reproduction. Both are made of oak splints.

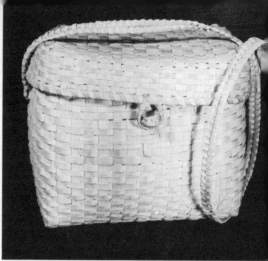

Trout basket with hinged lid. Made by Lottie Stamper with white oak splints.

Lady's over-the-shoulder bag. Made of white oak splints by Lottie Stamper.

Oak-splint shopping bag. Decorated with two colorful cross-stitch bands.

Colorful rib baskets. Also known as saddle, pack or bow baskets. This is not a traditional Cherokee shape, but has been made for many years by both white men and Indians of the Southern Highlands.

White oak rib baskets. Oval basket on left. Round basket with foot on right.

White oak basket. Design formed by alternating narrow and wide weaving splints.

White oak waste basket. Native dyes of blood root and walnut were used for some splints. Design is obtained by variation in width of splints. From the collection of the author.

Square to round white oak basket.

Wall or hanging baskets of white oak.

Market basket of white oak with carved handles.

Cherokee double-weave baskets. Basket on left is about one hundred years old. Basket on right is new and illustrates flowing water design.

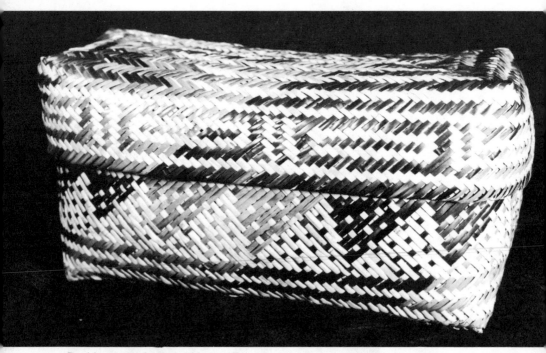

Double-weave basket with lid. This basket was reproduced from a photostatic copy of a Cherokee double-weave basket that has been in the British Museum since 1725. Basket is of split cane and is about eighteen inches long. Chief's coffin design on lid, arrow point design on body.

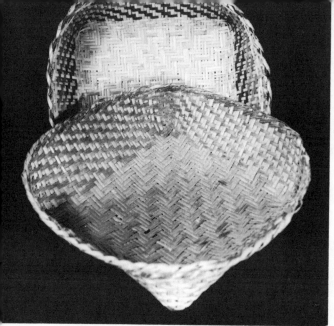

Cherokee bread baskets of native split cane. The one in foreground has been used for many years to drain chestnut bread and as a utility basket about the kitchen. The one in back is a recent reproduction.

Carrying basket of split cane. This was not strictly a Cherokee style but was typical of all Southeastern tribes. Hole in flap is a hand grip for use when basket is carried on the back.

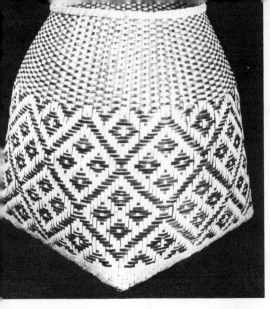

Burden or storage basket of cane. A large basket used by the Cherokee for carrying and storing grain. The big diamond design was used here. This shape is often used today for wastebaskets.

Barrel-shaped cane basket with chain and double chief's daughters designs.

Cane waste basket. Dyed with bloodroot and black walnut. Chain and cross-on-the-hill designs used.

DECORATION

The natural crossing of warps and weft elements in checkerwork, wickerwork and twilling produces pleasing patterns in itself, but the Cherokee add to the beauty of their baskets by the use of color and designs. Bold all-over patterns are worked into most of their ware. Naturally colored structural materials account for a good portion of the designs used on their baskets. Most baskets so decorated have a light background (the natural color of oak, cane or honeysuckle) on which appear designs in shades of black, brown, red, yellow, or any combination of these. These colored materials are part of the warp and weft elements that are dyed before the weaving starts.

When color is used, mosaic effects are produced in woven basketry. The tiny squares and rectangles formed by the crossing of elements can be arranged to produce an unlimited variety of patterns and effects. There is a possibility of variety even in checkerwork through changing the width of warp and weft elements. Oblong rectangles there mingle with tiny or larger squares in tassellated surfaces. When two colors are used, there is no limit to the possibilities any more than there is to the results an Italian workman may achieve when making a tessellated pavement with marble blocks in white and black.

As soon as the weaver steps outside of her monotonous checkerwork into the province of wicker, or especially twilled weaving, the possibilities of ornamentation are indefinitely multiplied. The elements of wickerwork mosaic are horizonal in the same piece. The Cherokee, by varying the twilling technique from over-two-under-two or over-five-under-five, have produced squares, triangles, rectangles, diamonds, crosses, lines, diagonals, zigzags, and chain patterns. Most of these patterns have been given names such as: chief's daughter, chief's coffin, big diamond, broken heart, and Indian arc. Although these names may have had symbolic meaning at an earlier date, they are used today merely for the convenience of identification.

Another type of decoration that is fairly common on Cherokee white oak baskets is made by twisting a weft strand into a curlicue or roll. The rolls are formed of strands, usually colored, inserted over another weft strand after the weaving is completed. A thin weft is drawn under a warp splint, given one or more turns either up or down, and the loose end drawn tightly under the next warp. This is continued around the basket and forms a row of projecting decorations.

USE AND QUALITY

Cherokee baskets, besides being attractive, are strong and serviceable. Some of their baskets have been in use from eighty to one hundred years and are still in good condition. Their waste baskets, marketbaskets, shopping baskets, picnic baskets, and sewing baskets are examples of useful baskets that fit well into the needs of every home. Some baskets the Indians formerly used, such as burden baskets, hominy sifters, and chestnut bread baskets, are in little demand and few are made today. The quality of Cherokee basketry and interest in this industrial art has steadily increased in recent years, and a great deal of pride in good craftsmanship exists among individual workers.

Market basket of native river cane.

Small waste basket of maple splints.

Cherokee cane mat, partially completed. Cross-on-the-hill pattern is being worked into an all-over design.

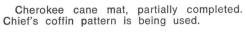

Cherokee cane mat, partially completed. Chief's coffin pattern is being used.

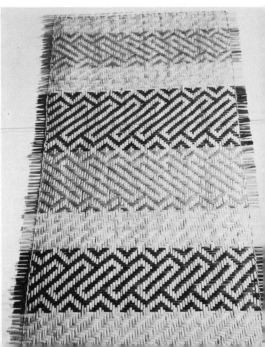

Cherokee cane mat with man-in-the-coffin pattern.

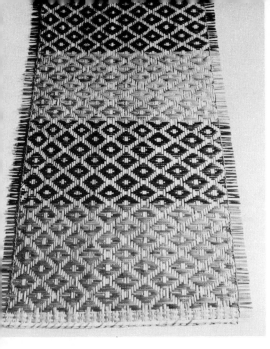

Cherokee cane mat with an all-over pattern of Chief's daughters.

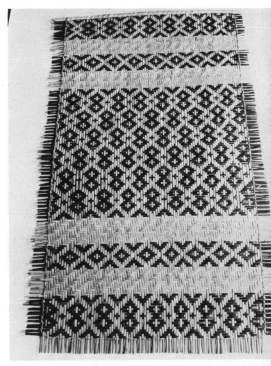

Cherokee cane mat using double Chief's daughters as the design element.

Cherokee cane mat. Design elements are diagonals and combinations of Chief's daughters.

Cherokee cane mat. Design elements are Chief's daughters and zigzags.

Cherokee cane mat. Broken-heart pattern is used in an all-over design.

Cherokee cane mat with Indian arc pattern.

Honeysuckle and oak rib waste basket with coiled design.

Honeysuckle mats and cut-flower basket. Mats are the natural white of skinned honeysuckle. The flower basket combines oak splits with natural and dyed honeysuckle.

Honeysuckle sewing baskets are usually made in two colors. This is the most popular shaped basket for which honeysuckle is used. Lids are always carefully fitted on these baskets.

Ladies' hand bag of honeysuckle and oak.

SOME CHEROKEE BASKETMAKERS

Mrs. Lottie Stamper has probably contributed more to the present day basketmaking skills and techniques of the Cherokee than any other one person. She learned oak splint basketry as a child from her mother and in 1935, at the age of 28, she started making cane baskets. In 1937, she started teaching basketmaking at the Cherokee School and over a period of many years taught hundreds of girls how to make baskets with oak, cane and honeysuckle. In 1940, Mrs. Stamper learned about the complex double-weave pattern from Mrs. Loineeta, an ancient of the tribe, and persuaded her to demonstrate the starting of such a basket. With the assistance of a photograph of a Cherokee double-weave basket that has been in the British Museum since 1725, she was able to work out perfectly details for completing the basket. Through her guidance and instruction there are now ten to fifteen Cherokee who make the double-weave basket. Thus, this rare and difficult basket-weaving technique that was virtually lost for more than 100 years has been revived.

On February 23, 1952, Mrs. Stamper received the highest honor bestowed by the Southern Highland Handicraft Guild—honorary life membership for her contributions to crafts. Only seven persons had been recognized for this award up to that time and she was the first Indian to receive it.

In recent years, Mrs. Stamper has given guidance and instruction in all types of basketmaking at several demonstration-workshops held on the Reservation in cooperation with the Cherokee Agency of the Bureau of Indian Affairs. The author is grateful to Mrs. Stamper for much information on basket construction and for supplying materials for many photographs on this subject.

It would be difficult to list all of the skilled basketmakers on the Cherokee Reservation, so only a few will be mentioned.

The late Mrs. Henry Bradley and the late Lizzie Youngbird were well-known for many years for their beautiful cane baskets. Other basketmakers who specialize in richly patterned river cane baskets are Mrs. Alice Walkingstick, who

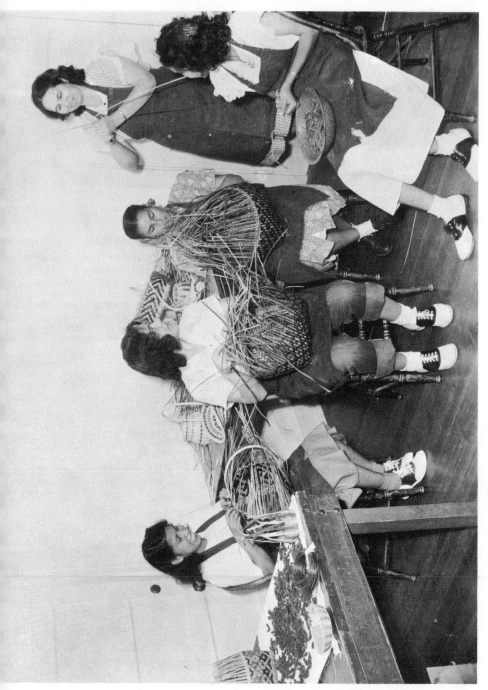

Mrs. Lottie Stamper and some of her students when she taught basketry at the Cherokee School.

demonstrates basketmaking at Oconaluftee Indian Village; Mrs. Eva Wolfe, who was honored with a display of eighteen of her baskets during December, 1969, at the Qualla Arts and Crafts Mutual Headquarters; Miss Carol Smith, who has assisted with some of the basketry demonstration-workshops on the Reservation; Elizabeth Brown Jackson and Emmaline Jackson Garrett.

Some craftsmen producing white oak splint baskets are Mrs. Elsie Welch Watty, Mrs. Amanda Smoker, Mrs. Bessie George Littlejohn and Mrs. Agnes Lossie Welch, while Mrs. Julie Taylor and Rachel Taylor specialize in white oak rib basketry.

Among those working in honeysuckle wicker basketry, an incomparable talent is shown by Mrs. Lucy George, who has received wide acclaim for the classic precision and perfection of her work. She received special recognition during May and June, 1970, when an exhibition of her honeysuckle baskets was on display at the Qualla Arts and Crafts Mutual, Inc., in Cherokee.

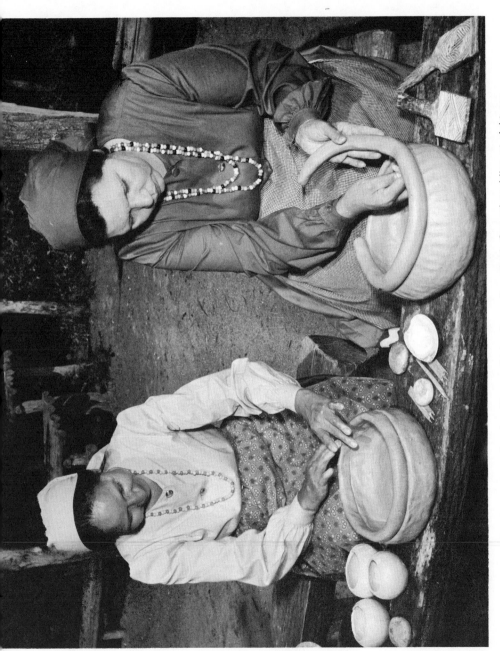

Cherokee potters forming large pots by the coil method. Carved paddles at right are used to stamp outter surface of ware. Oconaluftee Indian Village. Courtesy Cherokee Historical Association.

POTTERY

Of all the products of aboriginal handicraft, that of ceramics probably affords the best opportunity for the study of early stages in the evolution of art and in defining the geographic limitations and migrations of vanished peoples. The reasons for this may be stated briefly as follows: first, the need of vessels is common to all mankind, and the use of clay in vessel making is almost universal among the peoples sufficiently advanced to utilize it; second, since the clay used readily receives the impress of individual thought and skill the stamp of each people is distinctly impressed upon its ceramic products; third, the baked clay is permanently hardened, while at the same time it is so fragile that fragments remain in plenty at every site occupied by the pottery makers; fourth, vessels are less than all other articles fitted for and subject to transportation, being the most sedentary, so to speak, of all minor artifacts.

Fired clay pottery has been found in abundance at all sites investigated in the Cherokee area. The variety of size, shape, and method of decoration shows excellence in ceramic art at an early date.

Cherokee ware is made of native clay that takes on a variety of colors when subjected to heat ranging through gray, drab, yellow, red, brown, and sand. This results in the surface appearing blotchy. The deep gray or black of some pieces is due to wood smoke, and it was from this that the Cherokee learned the technique of firing their earthenware in a thick smudge to give it an even black tone. Some vessels still retain a black tinge on their inner surfaces due to the process used to render them impervious, and the exterior is sometimes coated with soot from the ancient campfires.

Cherokee potter making small pieces by hand. Oconaluftee Indian Village. Courtesy Cherokee Historical Association.

The surface of prehistoric ware, even when not purposely roughened, is seldom very smooth, and the texture is usually quite coarse, owing to a heavy admixture of pounded mussel-shells (Tennessee River area); sand and crushed stone (Nacoochee Mound in northern Georgia); and quartzite and mica (Etowah Mounds in Bartow County, Georgia) used in tempering. A few fragments, however, of especially well made bowls of fine texture and with a smooth polished surface on both sides, show that a better class of ware was known.

Although the esthetic idea was considerably developed among all classes of our aborigines, and much attention was paid to embellishment, it is not probable that any vessel was manufactured for purely ornamental purposes. The uses to which the earthenware of the aborigines was applied were numerous and important; they may be classed roughly as domestic, industrial, sacerdotal, ornamental, and trivial or diversional. To the first class belong vessels for containing, cooking, boiling, eating, drinking, etc; to the second belong various implements used in the arts, as trowels and modeling tools; to the third class belong vessels and other articles used in funeral rites, as burial urns and offerings; as personal ornaments there are beads, pendants, and earplugs; and for trivial and diversional uses there are toy vessels, figurines, and gaming articles. Most of the objects may serve a number of uses, as, for example, a single vessel may answer for culinary, for religious, and for mortuary purposes, and tobacco pipes may have ceremonial as well as medical and diversional uses. Articles of clay suited to all of the uses just mentioned were found on Cherokee sites.

Prehistoric Cherokee vessels have usually a round or somewhat conical base, which suggest the manner of their use. Hard, level floors were the exception, while floors of sand or soft earth were the rule; and under such conditions a round or conical base would be more convenient. The pot in cooking was generally set directly on the fire and was kept in position by the fuel or other supports placed about its sides.

Cherokee ware is found in a variety of forms which may

be classed as pot-like forms, bowls, bottles, and effigy vessels. It varies in thickness from one-tenth to seven-tenths of an inch, with an average of about three-tenths; and in size from less than an inch in diameter to more than three feet in diameter. As a rule, the walls are surprisingly thin and we must admire the skill of the potter who could execute vessels of large size and fine proportions with walls at no point exceeding three-eights of an inch in thickness. The most characteristic design element of the Cherokee area is the curving scroll appearing in many forms from the tight spiral to bands of parrallel irregularly flowing lines. Decoration is produced by incising, which is done freehand with a pointed instrument on the clay while still soft; by stamping it with a carved paddle; by imprinting it with the end of some kind of hollow cylinder such as a quill or a piece of cane; and by dots produced by pressing a solid point into the clay. A body-finish was effected by strokes of a carved paddle or one wrapped with cord; by brushing with a bundle of stiff grass; or, in the case of the coarse basins or vats of the salt-pan type, by constructing the vessel in a hole lined with pieces of native fabric which left its imprint on the finished product. Some vessels were left plain and a few examples of painted ware have been found.

There seems to be no rule that certain forms carry certain modes of embellishment. One form may be decorated in several ways, or a jar may be finished with a combination of designs each differing from the other in technique of execution—incising, stamping and molding. Feet, handles, lugs, and ears were common. The handles were usually flat and often decorated.

The shaping processes employed in vessel making were chiefly modeling and molding. Although the molding process was much used in archaic times, it alone was never competent to complete a utensil; the plastic clay had to be squeezed into the mold and was therefore shaped, on one side at least, by modeling with the fingers or an implement. On the other hand, modeling alone was capable of accomplishing every necessary part of the shaping and finishing of vessels.

Early Cherokee pottery. The scribed designs shown were typical of all Southeastern tribes as well as the Cherokee. The flat handles on bowl at left are also typical of this area.

Effigy bowls often depicted frogs, turtles, birds, animals and human beings. Museum of the Cherokee Indian. Cherokee, North Carolina.

Effigy jugs were rare among the Cherokee, and few whole jugs have been found. Museum of the Cherokee Indian, Cherokee, North Carolina.

Cherokee pots of this shape were used for many purposes. Small ones were used for cooking. The rounded bottom made it possible for the pot to sit level on the campfire or in the sand. Large pots held the bodies of children for burial. These were always killed (broken by knocking a hole in the bottom) so the pot could go to the next world with the child. Museum of the Cherokee Indian, Cherokee, North Carolina.

Rare chestnut burr pots. Only a few such types are known and they are all Cherokee patterns. Museum of the Cherokee Indian, Cherokee, North Carolina.

Early Cherokee pottery designs. Reproduced from **Decorative Art and Basketry of the Cherokee** by Frank G. Speck by permission of the Public Museum of the City of Milwaukee.

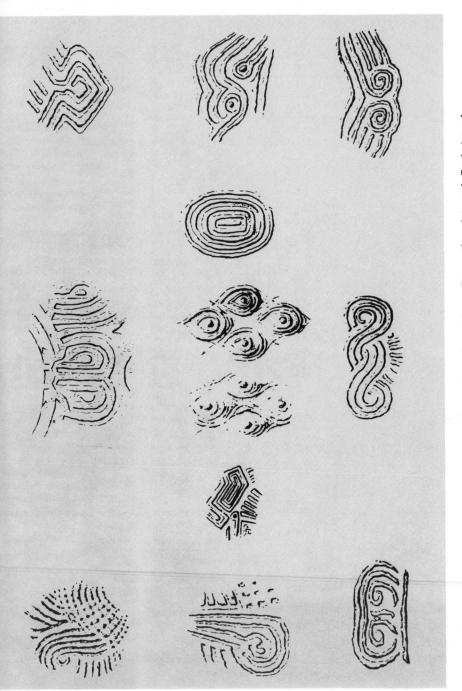

More Cherokee pottery designs. Reproduced from **Decorative Art and Basketry of the Cherokee** by Frank G. Speck by permission of the Public Museum of the City of Milwaukee.

Cherokee pottery designs from rims. Reproduced from **Decorative Art and Basketry of the Cherokee** by Frank G. Speck, by permission of the Public Museum of the City of Milwaukee.

M. R. Harrington, who studied a skillful Cherokee potter practicing the art on the Qualla reservation in 1908, reports the following account of the processes involved, which probably are practically the same as in prehistoric times and give us a better picture of their manufacturing technique:

"Mr. James Mooney had given me the name of one potter, Iwi Katalsta, and I lost no time in making her acquaintance. Inquiry resulted in the discovery of but one more, an aged woman known as Jennie Arch, whose feeble hands had all but lost their skill. For this reason I confined myself almost entirely to Iwi's methods of pottery-making. Fully half the pottery I secured from the Eastern Cherokee is said to be the work of her hand.

"Her tools were few, and with one exception, simple, consisting of a hammerstone for pounding the clay, a sharpened bit of stick for making lines and notches, and a fine-grained, waterworn pebble for smoothing, showing the polish of long use. The exception is the carved paddle for stamping the pottery—a broad bladed wooden affair about eight inches long, carefully carved to produce a checkerwork pattern when struck against soft clay. More paddles bearing different figures were later collected, some quite complex. Other accessories were a common axe, a bucket of water, a low-sided wooden tray for kneading clay, and a flat, oval piece of wood used as a stand to build large jars upon and provided with a handle at each end for convenience in turning; some saucers of china or gourd, and some pieces of cotton sheeting.

"After Iwi Katalsta had dug her clay from a bed on Soco Creek, the exact location of which she did not seem inclined to reveal, she was accustomed to mold it into a cake some fourteen inches long, resembling in form a loaf of bread, in which shape it was dried and laid away for future use. When we visited her home at 'Yellow Hill' and requested her to make us some pottery, she broke off the end of this cake and proceeded to pulverize it on her hearthstone, using the back of a common axe as a crushing instrument. In old times, she explained, a 'long rock' was used for this purpose.

"When sufficiently pulverized, the clay was placed in a

wooden tray, moistened and again thoroughly pounded. This time Iwi used a hammerstone which she kept especially to crush hickory nuts, but which she often used in place of the axe in pounding the dampened clay. From time to time the mass was kneaded and a little more water or dry clay added as seemed necessary to obtain the required consistency. Sometimes, I was informed, a fine sand was added at this stage as a tempering material; but in this case it was omitted.

"Iwi had a vessel of the pot form in mind. Taking a large handful of the clay, she patted it into a ball, which she took in both hands and pressing her thumbs deeply into one side, began to turn it rapidly. In a surprisingly short time a small bowl with fairly thin sides was produced to serve as a base for the future vessel. During this process she had taken care to keep her hands wet. Then supporting the inside of the bowl with the fingers of her left hand she struck it sharply on the outside with her carved paddle, slightly turning the embryo vessel before each stroke and moistening the paddle now and then in a vessel of water which stood near. The bowl-shaped base was then carefully laid upon a bit of cotton cloth resting on a common china saucer. When questioned as to what the Indians used before saucers were available, Iwi replied through the interpreter that she had heard that for large vessels the base was set in a hole in the sand lined with some sort of cloth, the sand being often enclosed in a basket for convenience. For small vessels, she said, a saucer made of gourd was just as serviceable as one of china, and as I liked the old style, she would take care to use gourd supports hereafter in making pottery for me. It was her custom, she continued, when making the large, flat-bottomed hominy jars to set the base on the oval, flat utensil of wood before mentioned, especially made for the purpose and provided with a handle at each end to facilitate turning.

"The bowl-shaped base having been safely esconced in the saucer she pinched its edges thin with wet fingers; then, rapidly rolling out a lump of clay on a plank into a long thin cylinder, she applied it just inside the rim of the base and projecting above it about half its width, pinching it fast the while until the circuit was completed. The coil proved a bit too long, so she broke the superflous piece off and blended the two ends together with care. Then by careful pinching and smoothing with wet fingers and fingernails, the coil was blended with the bowl-shaped base and thinned at the top to receive another coil which was also applied inside. The object of applying each coil inside instead of directly on top of the preceding was to produce strength by overlapping. Thus the coiling preceeded until the required form and height were reached, when the rim coil was applied outside the one beneath. After being blended in the usual way, this was pinched into lateral protuberances, and notched, dotted, or marked with a shapened stick to suit the fancy. After each coil had been applied and blended, the vessel was allowed to dry and harden a few minutes before the next one was added; and after the jar had received its shape, it was allowed to become quite firm before the final stamping was applied.

"It will be remembered that the base of the vessel had already been stamped before being placed in the saucer, so it was now necessary only to strike the body briskly with the wet paddle until the surface was covered with its imprints. In one jar the stamping was complete before the rim was added. After stamping, the vessel was set away to dry.

"The fact that Iwi used no tools except the paddle, the marking stick and her fingers, seemed remarkable to me, in view of the numerous smoothing tools of gourd, shell, bone, and wood, employed by the Catawba. Inquiry revealed the fact that while they had apparently never heard of gourd smoothers, the Cherokee formerly used musselshells and a marine shell, probably some species of Cardium, for this purpose. Iwi herself sometimes used a chip of wood in making large vessels.

"After drying,—a process that takes from one to three days, depending on the weather,—the vessel was carefully rubbed and polished on the inside, and on the outside whenever necessary, with the smoothing stone kept wet by continual dipping in water.

"When a number of vessels had been made and dried,

the next step was to prop the vessels up on their sides a-round the fire, mouth toward the blaze, until a faint brown color, beginning near the fire, crept over the whole of the vessels—a sign that they were hot enough for firing. Then the potter, with a long stick, rolled them over, mouth-down, upon the embers, and covered them with pieces of dry bark to the depth of two or three inches. Making sure that the bark had caught fire all around, she left them to their fate. About an hour later the bark had burned away, leaving the rounded bottoms of the pots protruding through the ashes. Then, tak-ing her long hooked stick, Iwi rolled the vessels from the fire, tapping them sharply to detect cracks. If the vessel rang clear it was perfect.

"In order to be good for cooking, these pots should be smoked she said. 'If this is not done, the water will soak through.' So she dropped a handful of bran in each one while they were still almost red-hot, stirred it with her stick, tipped the pots this way and that, and finally, turning out the now blazing bran from each in turn, inverted the vessels upon it. In this way, the inside was smoked black and rend-ered impervious, and this without leaving any odor of smoke in the vessels when they became cold. Generally, Iwi told me, crushed corncobs were employed for this purpose, but she always used bran when cobs were not available. This prob-ably explains the black color of the inner surface so often seen in aboriginal pottery.

"I was told that in later times the firing has been general-ly done indoors, because an absolutely still day was necesary for a successful burning in the open air, any breeze being liable to crack the vessels. The firing of my pottery was, how-ever, done outdoors, the fire being built on a rude hearth of flat stones sunk level with the ground."

Lieutenant Timberlake reports that the Cherokee also made fine pipes of pottery ware. He says he almost suffo-cated with the great number of peace pipes he had to smoke as a pledge of friendship.

Timberlake also noted that the Cherokee "have two sorts of clay, red and white, with both of which they make excellent vessels, some of which will stand the greatest heat." Adair said, "They make earthen pots of very different sizes, so as to contain from two to ten gallons; large pitchers to carry water; bowls, dishes, platters, basons, and a prodicious number of other vessels of such antiquated forms, as would be tedious to describe, and impossible to name. Their method of glazing them, is, they place them over a large fire of smoky pitch pine, which makes them smooth, black, and firm. Their lands abound with proper clay, for that use; and even with porcelain, as has been proved by experiment."

Further evidence as to the high quality of the Cherokee clay is attested by the fact that in 1767 Thomas Griffiths, a native of England and sometime resident of Charleston, South Carolina, was commissioned by the talented English potter, Josiah Wedgewood, to investigate the clay pits of Western North Carolina. The white men had learned that the Cherokee Indians were using a fine white clay for their pottery and it was Griffiths' duty to secure some of this clay for Wedgewood, who was then starting to develop a beautiful blue and white jasper ware. Griffiths received permission from the Cherokee to dig in the clay pits and, after enduring many difficulties and hardships, he took five tons of the clay. Wedgewood ware has often been imitated, but none has equalled Wedgewood's first pieces into which he put his "Cherokee Clay" from Western North Carolina. On August 11, 1959, the North Carolina State Department of Archives and History unveiled a historical maker on N. C. Highway 28, a few miles north of Franklin in Macon County, to designate the pit from which the "Cherokee Clay" was obtained.

Some pottery techniques of the Cherokee are presumed to be of Catawba origins, although the clays of course, are from the Cherokee area. In 1840 about one hundred Catawba, nearly all that were left of the tribe, being dissatisfied with their conditions in South Carolina, moved up in a body and took up their residence with the Cherokee. Latent tribal jealousies broke out, however, and at their own request negotiations were begun in 1848 for their removal to Indian Territory. The effort being without results, they soon began to drift back to their own homes, until in 1852, there were only about a dozen remaining among the Cherokee. In 1890, only one was left, an old woman, the widow of a Cherokee. She and her daughter, both of whom spoke the Cherokee language, were expert potters according to the Catawba method, which differs markedly from that of the Cherokee.

Notes made by Mary Ulmer Chiltoskey, former librarian at the Cherokee School, at an interview with Mrs. Lula Owle Gloyne, great niece of Suzanna Harris, one of the outstanding Catawba pottery makers living among the Eastern Cherokee, give us some information on both the original Cherokee pottery and the Catawba pottery.

A piece of original Cherokee pottery bought by Mr. Gloyne, several years before his death, is now in the Smithsonian Institution. This piece was made by Mrs. Eva Catolster, the last of the original pottery makers who made pottery until her death in 1907.

Mrs. Gloyne told about visiting Mrs. Catolster to see pottery being made. "Some people may tell you that this is not authenic, but I'll tell you what I saw with my own eyes," said Mrs. Gloyne. "The pottery was buried in the ground and fired four days, using charcoal, corncobs, and corn for fuel. The pieces of pottery were packed with bark in such manner as to prevent the pieces from touching as they fell during the firing. The corn helped to produce the black splotches that are typical of Cherokee pottery. The charcoal that she used was made from native woods burned in a hole dug out of the side of a hill. This pottery would hold water and was used for cooking."

Then Mrs. Gloyne began to think and tell about the coming of the Catawba influence into the pottery making of the Cherokee. "The Harris women, one of whom was Lula's mother, brought some of these ideas to Cherokee with them when they married Cherokee men and came to Cherokee to live." Lula continued with her narrative: "When Sampson Owle married Suzanne Harris, a Catawba, the Catawba type of pottery making was brought to the Cherokees. This pottery has taken the place of the original Cherokee ware for selling to tourists.

"I can remember my mother and Aunt Suzanna baking pottery before the fire in the house. The pieces were placed in a semicircle on the hearth. As the pieces began to heat, they were pushed gradually closer and turned. As they got close to the fire, tongs were used to handle them. When they were ready for intense heat, the ones to be blackened were placed in old square oil tins, packed with bark, and placed in the center of the fireplace. The pieces to be left 'natural' were placed around the outside. We children usually left home on the days that pottery was being burned because the house got so hot."

Within the memory of people still living, the Cherokee used pottery vessels for cooking, and some families still have cooking pots of pottery which bear the marks of the flames and smoke from the hearth fires where the cooking was done. When the Cherokee ceased using clay vessels to cook in, little pottery was made and there were only three potters left on the Reservation in 1890. Through the efforts of the Indian Arts and Crafts Board, there has been a revival of the craft. Cherokee potters are now conscientiously attempting to make their wares as much like the ancient Cherokee pottery as possible. Genuine Cherokee vessels were studied and fragments from Cherokee mounds were pieced together to give a true picture of the type of ware made by the Cherokee tribe in its palmy days before the removal of a majority of the tribe to the west. Pottery experts in the Indian Service and outstanding Cherokee artists worked together to make the reconstruction and revival possible.

The Cherokee formerly made all their pottery from native clay, but now much of it is made from commercial clays. The following incident reported in 1938 indicates how scarce native clay was at that time. "Recently a delegation from one of the churches on the Reservation came before the business committee of the tribal council and complained that pottery makers were undermining the church. Of course this source of supply had to be shut off by the committee."

Cherokee pottery is truly handmade, being formed en-

Carved pottery stamping paddles. Used by the early Cherokee to decorate the outer surface of their ware.

Cherokee pottery. The large peace pipe and chestnut burr pot are by Maude Welch. Wedding jug on left is by Ethel Big Meat. The miniature wash pot is unsigned. The black color is a result of baking in the fire boxes of their cook stoves. These pieces are from the collection of the author.

The late Maud Welch. Most of her life was spent making genuine Cherokee-style pottery. In this picture she is using a knife to shape a piece of her ware.

tirely by modeling without the use of a potter's wheel or slip molds. Large pieces are built by the coil methods and smaller ware is shaped from one ball of clay. A knife is generally used to whittle the roughly molded pot to a true balanced shape and the ware is next polished to a shiny finish with a smooth stone or tool. The pottery is then air dried in the sun or near the cook stove and is finished by burning in the fire box of the kitchen stove. This ware is not very hard and is too porous to hold water well, but, because of the traditional shapes and designs and the pleasing colors of dull black, mottled tan, pink and smoky black produced in firing, it finds a ready market. Although this potttery is unglazed, it has a shine which results from the careful polishing given each piece before firing. A few of the shapes the Cherokee make are vases, pots, bowls, wedding jugs and peace pipes.

Maude Welch was well known for her handmade, home-burned pottery on the Reservation. She was born near Cooper's Creek in the Birdtown section of the Reservation in 1894. In an interview with the writer before her death, Mrs. Welch explained that she had been making the Cherokee style pottery for over thirty years, and that she felt lost when not carving or polishing a piece of the ware. Mrs. Welch obtained clay for her first pieces from a neighbor and fired the finished products under her washpot. When she learned she could trade her pottery at the store for a sack of flour, some lard and a box of salt, she decided it was a good thing. Asked where she got the clay, she smiled and said, "Well you see, I used to dig it out of holes along Cooper's Creek and in Soco Valley, but I got so 'rheumaticky', I could not dig any more, to do any good, so I started ordering it from the pottery factories."

Among the pieces Mrs. Welch made were the traditional peace pipes, wedding jugs and medicine bowls. Mrs. Welch explained: "When the Medicine Man prescribes medicine for the Indians, he has them take one or two bowlfuls. That's what the medicine bowl is for." She learned to make the traditional Cherokee shapes from museum pieces, photographs, and information obtained from others on the Reser-

Cherokee pottery by Rebecca Amanda Youngbird. Stairway-to-Heaven design used on pot at left. Friendship design on center pot, and a variation of friendship design used on pot at right.

Cherokee pottery by Rebecca Amanda Youngbird. The process by which she blackens her ware is kept secret. Stairway-to-Heaven design is used on large pot; friendship design is used on pieces in center and lower left; center piece is a wedding jug which is always broken as part of the ceremony. Upper right piece is a Roman-style lamp used by the Cherokee to burn bear fat oil.

Cherokee corn pot. Authentic reproduction of an ancient Cherokee form and design. Stand is used, as pot has a rounded bottom for setting on fire while cooking. Corn design was impressed with a corn cob. Made in 1967 by Cora Wahnetah. From the collection of the author.

Recent Cherokee pottery vase with carved Indian heads.

Cherokee wedding jug. Blackware with friendship design.

Cherokee Madonna of terra cotta by Amanda Crowe.

vation; but, she added, "I polish them up smoother and add more designs so that people will buy them." Her polishing stone was smoother than glass and had been used for over twenty-five years.

Mrs. Welch said, "I attended the Southern Guild Fair, and I learned how other pottery makers used kilns for the burning of their pieces. I decided that I would try to make mine that way, but the people didn't want it. They said mine were different—the only pieces of the kind anywhere—so, I decided to hang on to the old way, not to modernize." Mrs. Welch used no wheels, molds, or instruments other than small knives, in the shaping of her pottery. She turned the pieces out entirely by hand, dried them in the sun and in the oven of her stove, and then dropped them into the fire box for the finishing touch of color.

The Cherokee have been pottery makers from the earliest times, although there were periods when only a few members of the tribe practiced the art. Presently there are a number of skilled Cherokee potters on the Reservation turning out traditional ware. The styles and designs used are authentic and their methods of forming, decorating and firing are the same as those used by their ancestors.

Rebecca Youngbird, Cora Wahnetah, Lizzie Bigmeat Jackson and Edith Welch Bradley are well known for the high quality of the Cherokee pottery they are currently producing.

WOODCRAFTS

Although few examples of early projects in wood remain, due to decay, woodwork has always been highly regarded among the Cherokee. Adair wrote in 1775 "Their stools they cut out of poplar wood, all of one piece, and of a convenient height and shape. Their chests are made of clapboards sewed to cross bars with scraped wet buffalo strings . . . Their wooden dishes, and spoons made of wood and buffalo horn, show something of a newer invention and date, being of nicer workmanship for the sculpture of the last is plain and represents things that are within the reach of their own ideas."

The Cherokee are known to have made dugout canoes from large, straight poplar logs. Trees used were often more than two hundred years old. They were hollowed out by alternately burning, scraping and chipping. A stone adze was used for scraping and chipping before white man introduced metal tools. Many canoes were thirty to forty feet long but they were not excessively heavy or clumsy. They were often wider than two feet and had a depth of about one foot. Considerable skill is evident in the fact that the walls were only one or two inches thick. Visitors to the reservation can witness this ancient craft being demonstrated at the Oconoluftee Indian Village.

The early Cherokee carved intricate geometrical designs on their wooden pottery paddles used for stamping the outer surface of much of their ceramic ware. They also carved eleborate designs of snakes and animals on their long wooden pipestems. Low relief carvings of animals were used to decorate the surface of their drums which were hollowed out of buckeye. The ends of these hollowed log sections were

Cherokee man making dugout canoe from large poplar log. Oconaluftee Indian Village. Courtesy Cherokee Historical Association.

Cherokee craftsman carving booger mask from buckeye. Oconaluftee Indian Village. Courtesy Cherokee Historical Association.

Carved rattlesnake mask. Made by Allen Long, son of the famous Medicine Man and mask-maker Will West Long. Displayed at the Cherokee Indian Fair.

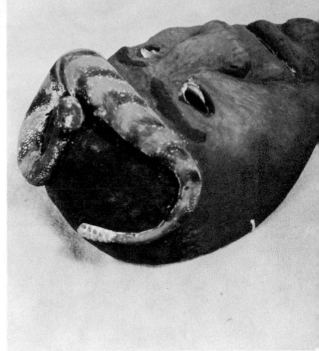

Masks by Will West Long, the last rather famous Cherokee Medicine Man. Used in ceremonial dances and when treating the sick. Carved from poplar wood and decorated with bear skin and woodchuck hair, dyed with sassafras and red earth. Mask on left represents the devil; mask in center was used in the Ghost Dance; mask on right was a favorite of the Medicine Man when treating the sick. All are over seventy years old and are part of a mask collection in The Museum of the Cherokee Indian, Cherokee, North Carolina.

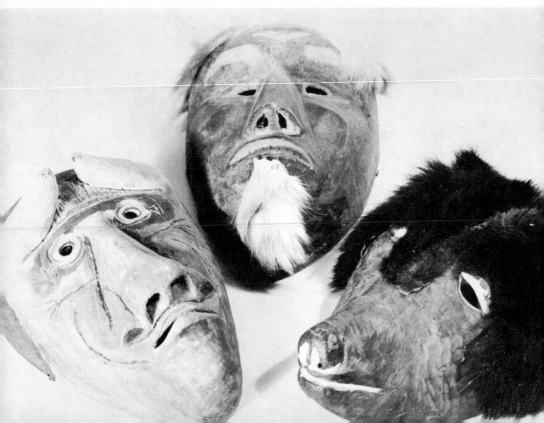

usually covered with groundhog skin. Sometimes the log was not hollowed all the way through and was partially filled with water to give a variety of tones according to the depth of the water.

Another form of early Cherokee wood carving was the "Willum Ollum" (carved wood totem). This was in the form of a long pole on which was carved a pictoral history of each chief of the Cherokee. This form of carving was lost to them during the Colonial period.

Masks carved from wood by Medicine Men are used during dances and on various ceremonial occasions. These were formerly made for the Indians' use and were seldom found for sale in the craft shops, but in recent years more have been made for sale to the public. A group of these masks carved by Medicine Man Will West Long may be seen in the Museum of the Cherokee Indian, Cherokee, North Carolina. Some of these masks resemble snakes, bears, and other animals and are ornamented with fur or horns. Cherokee masks are usually carved from soft wood such as buckeye or poplar but sometimes the Medicine Man will use hornets' nests, gourds or any other material at hand in their construction.

The Cherokee make ball sticks which are used in the unique sport "Indian Stickball". The sticks, shaped somewhat like small tennis rackets, are made of hickory and strung with rawhide thongs. A tiny walnut-sized, leather-covered ball is used with the sticks to play the game. The object of the game is to carry or throw the ball between the goal a dozen times. The goal line is marked by two willow sticks on a field 100 yards long. Each side has ten players. The battle begins when the Medicine Man tosses the ball into the air between the captains of the two teams. They jump and and try to hit the ball toward the goal. Players are not allowed to pick up the ball with their hands, but must use sticks. Once they pick up the ball with their sticks, they carry it in their hands or in their mouth. Anything goes—biting and choking, gouging and scratching, twisting arms and legs— even banging each other on the head with their wooden rackets. There are no time-outs, no substitutions, and no time limits. If a player is knocked out—and they often are—his opponent must also leave the game. Twenty men may start a game and only a few finish it. The first team that has twelve counting pegs stuck into the ground by the Medicine Man wins the ball game. Once entire villages played the game to settle arguments among the clans; now, however, the game is a sporting event. There is a historic incident whereby a land dispute between two tribes was settled peaceably on the ball field. In olden days, Indians gathered from miles around to watch the games and to bet anything they possessed on their favorite team. It was not at all uncommon for a man to go home after the game minus both his horse and his shirt.

The men of the tribe have always been the wood-carvers. From large pieces of native wood—such as cherry or walnut—they gouge, carve, and finish handsome wooden bowls. These oblong, hand-carved bowls of various sizes have been judged by the National Indian Arts and Crafts Board to be an outstanding achievement in craftwork. Several of these bowls are now serving as museum pieces. Cherokee wood-carvers have found that their salad forks and spoons, bookends, salt and pepper shakers, plates, and boxes are always popular craft items. Cherokee men especially enjoy whittling or carving animals. Besides walnut and cherry they use buckeye, holly, apple and other native woods. These lifelike and amusing carvings represent the creatures of the forest as well as domesticated animals. A natural finish applied to the many native woods used produces a wide variety of colors and wood textures. These animals are often grouped to form an interesting barnyard or forest scene.

Other articles which the Cherokee wood-carvers make for their own use and for sale to the tourist include: carved and painted canes, bows, arrows, quivers, napkin rings, paper knives and carved pins. The jointed Indian character dolls, carved by the men and dressed by their wives, are always charming and especially popular with children.

Although men have traditionally been the wood-carvers,

undoubtedly the most influential carver on the Cherokee Reservation today is Miss Amanda Crowe. She received her Master of Fine Arts degree at the Chicago Art Institute and has taught woodcarving in the Cherokee Indian School for a number of years. Miss Crowe is perhaps best known for her small scale animal carvings which exhibit great charm and warmth. Her works have been widely shown in museum and gallery exhibitions throughout the country. In great part due to Miss Crowe's inspiration, the craftsmen of the Cherokee Reservation have attained considerable renown for the individuality and unique quality of their wood carvings.

Cherokee men learn woodcraft either from their fathers or in the Cherokee school. The educational program on the Reservation began in 1883 with the establishment of an industrial school and other common schools. The high school, which was accredited in 1941, offers the regular required courses that lead toward graduation in addition to boys' and girls' vocational work. Graduates of the high school enter colleges or schools for special training if they wish. Many Cherokee attend Western Carolina University, located at Cullowhee, North Carolina, only twenty-five miles from the Reservation, where major programs in Fine and Industrial Arts as well as academic subjects are offered.

Going Back Chiltoskey, who is without doubt one of the leading artist-craftsmen of the tribe, was for years in charge of the high school woodshop. The writer has known Chiltoskey for many years, and in a recent interview obtained some interesting sidelights on his early life. Going Back was born in 1907 in the Piney Grove section of the Reservation. Neither of his parents spoke English and he did not learn to speak it until, at the age of ten, he attended the Reservation school. Chiltoskey said that he had been interested in arts, crafts, and mechanical things all his life. As a boy, he sketched the moutain scenes about him and with his knife he whittled and carved his friends of the forest from pieces of laurel, cherry, or holly. He was always able to secure a little candy money by selling some of his whittlings. Going Back never owned bought toys, but constructed his own. One

Going Back Chiltoskey, versatile Cherokee craftsman, is shown in his shop working on one of his woodcarvings. This picture was made in 1952 when he taught woodcrafts at the Cherokee School.

Cherokee mother by Going Back Chiltoskey. Carved of native wild cherry. The piece is about thirty years old and has aged to a mellow dark red color. Cherokee women still use this method to carry their babies. Museum of the Cherokee Indian, Cherokee, North Carolina.

Woodcarvings in the Museum of the Cherokee Indian. Center figure was carved by Going Back Chiltoskey and represents his brother Watty Chiltoskey carving a pair of horsehead book ends. Figure on right is a Cherokee woman grinding corn into meal with a wooden mortar.

Amanda Crowe, outstanding Cherokee craftsman, working on large wood sculpture. Courtesy Cherokee Historical Association.

Cherokee dough bowls. Gouged from large pieces of native wild cherry. This style bowl as been recognized as an outstanding craft achievement by the National Indian Arts and Crafts Board, and several have been purchased for museum pieces.

Salad set of native wild cherry. Bowls are gouged and carved to the shape of old-fashioned dough bowls. Courtesy Indian Arts and Crafts Board.

Eagle Dancer by John J. Wilnoty. This 27-inch high figure is carved from one solid piece of native wild cherry.

Eagle Dancer — rear view.

of his favorites was the toy water wheels which he would build along the tumbling streams. He would use a thread for a belt to transmit his harnessed water power to other mechanical toys. As he grew up, he learned the carpentry trade and helped construct many of the present buildings on the Cherokee Indian Agency grounds. He received further education at the Parker High School, Greenville, South Carolina; The Haskel Institute, Lawrence, Kansas, where he graduated; and the Santa Fe Indian School in New Mexico, where he specialized in arts and crafts, furniture making, and jewelry making.

In 1927 Chiltoskey became associated with Boy Scout work in Greenville, South Carolina. His interest in young people prompted him to spend many of his summers as a counselor in Indian crafts at camps for boys and girls in the states of South Carolina, Pennsylvania, Massachusetts and Colorado. Going Back's desire for travel and adventure led him to join a reptile exhibition show that went under the name of White Eagle. The show had its ups and downs as it traveled north through Washington, D. C. and other cities, and was finally disbanded in Baltimore.

Chiltoskey became an instructor at the Qualla School in Cherokee in 1935 and remained there until he went to work for the War Department in 1942. During the next four and a half years he served his country as a model maker for the Army Engineers at Fort Belvoir, Virginia. He worked on maps, tank parts, experiments with plastics, and a very complex launching bridge. At the conclusion of World War II, Chiltoskey went into business in Hollywood, California, with three associates. They constructed architects' models of buildings, sets for movies, store displays, and projects of a similar nature. After about nine months in Hollywood, Going Back's desire to return to the beautiful valleys at the foot of the Great Smokies caused him to sell his interest in the business and return to the land of his birth, where he again became a member of the staff at the Qualla School.

Chiltoskey's wide training, experience, and native ability have made him a versatile artist with many media. His skills in cabinet-making, woodcarving, jewelry making, pencil sketching, and water color painting have won much praise. His work has been displayed in Cherokee, Gatlinburg, and Knoxville, and he has contributed much to the training of other craftsmen on the Reservation. His brother, Watty Chiltoskey, and his nephews, William Crowe and Richard Crowe, who are outstanding woodcarvers, were among his pupils. Hundreds of visitors to the Smoky Mountain National Park have had the opportunity of watching Chiltoskey demonstrate his ability in relief carving at the Southern Highlanders Handicraft Fair in recent years. Going Back Chiltoskey no longer teaches at the school, but he continues to produce excellent craft articles. He is an inspiration to Cherokee artists and craftsmen.

John J. Wilnoty of the Wolftown section of the Cherokee Reservation is considered by the Indian Arts and Crafts Board of Washington, D. C., to be the finest primitive stone and wood sculptor in America today. He has never had an art course or lesson, yet his pieces are on display in major museums and collections throughout the United States. His carvings in wild cherry, walnut and buckeye are pure masterpieces.

Wilnoty has little formal education, but had a burning wish to possess some talent with which to make a living for himself and his family. This came in a God-given sense of proportion and balance in his carvings. Never duplicating himself in the exact, he may use the same subjects over and over. He derives great pleasure in "hiding" smaller designs of birds and other animals within the figures of larger ones. Collectors may purchase a piece of his work and months later, upon closer inspection, find all kinds of tiny figures clearly visible within the features of the work.

The Eagle Dancer is considered by Wilnoty and its present owner, Thomas B. Underwood of Cherokee, himself a noted authority on Indian arts and crafts, to be his finest work. Hundreds of people have come to view the 27-inch high figure since it has been on display at the Medicine Man Gift Shop at Cherokee. The Eagle Dancer is carved from one

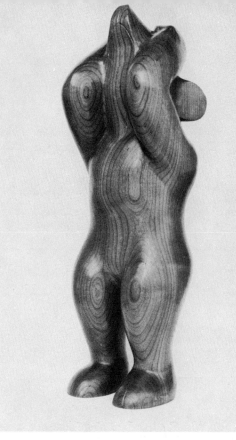

Howling fox carved from native wild cherry. Carved by Amanda Crowe.

Frustrated bear carved from native wild cherry. Carved by Amanda Crowe.

Bear cubs carved from black walnut.

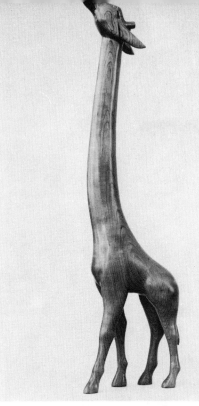

Standing bear carved from black walnut by Amanda Crowe. This standing position is often assumed by the black bears in the Great Smoky Mountain National Park adjoining the Cherokee Reservation.

Giraffe carved from native wild cherry by Boyce Allison. Courtesy Indian Arts and Crafts Board.

Cherokee woodcarvings. The cow is carved from native holly and the pigs from wild cherry.

Wild Geese carved from buckeye.

Swans carved from native wild cherry by Freeman Owle. Courtesy Indian Arts and Crafts Board.

Raccoon carved from buckeye.

Owls come in all sizes.
Carved from buckeye.

Quail carved from buck-
eye.

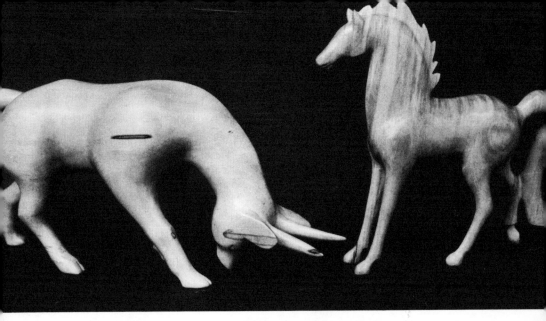

Antelope and colt carved from buckeye.

Woodcarvings by Mose Owl. The rackets are used in the Cherokee Indian ball game, often called the roughest sport in the world. The quiver is hollowed out of one piece of wood. Snake on walking stick is part of the same piece as the walking stick itself.

Wooden dolls. Hand carved from wild cherry with movable arms. Carving is done by the men and dolls are dressed by the women.

Cherokee dolls grinding corn in an old-time wooden mortar.

solid piece of native wild cherry and took approximately two months of steady work by Wilnoty. The pose represents an eagle in the ceremonial victory dance universally performed by Indians all over the country. Wilnoty has utilized the grain of the cherry wood to represent the body form of the subject. The perfection with which the pose is placed to work with the grain is almost unbelievable. It appears as if Wilnoty had taken the grain and worked the layers of the muscles of the body so that he constructed a perfect man, poised in a dramatic movement of the dance.

In addition to Amanda Crowe, Going Back Chiltoskey and John J. Wilnoty, the following Cherokee woodcarvers have received recognition for their originality and skill: Virgil Ledford, James A. Bradley, John R. Bradley, Richard Crowe, William Crowe and Lee Arch.

Much progress has been made in both the quality and design of woodcarved items produced on the Cherokee Reservation in recent years, and it is now recognized as one of their major crafts.

Cherokee woman practicing the centuries-old art of finger weaving. Only here has this tedious, forgotten art been preserved. Oconaluftee Indian Village. Courtesy Cherokee Historical Association.

WEAVING

Because cloth rots, it is found only in unusual circumstances, such as preservation in dry caves or by salts from contact with adjacent objects of copper. There is ample evidence, however, to indicate that woven textiles in North America are at least twenty-five hundred years old and may be among the oldest arts in the New World. Women pottery makers often impressed the soft surface of the molded vessel with a woven garment or blanket before placing it in the fire to harden. Careful scrutiny of these impressions indicates a great variety of weaving techniques. Evidence indicates that a variety of materials were used in textiles, mainly fibre of bark, flax, hemp, nettles, and grasses which were spun into thread of various sizes; or of splints of wood, twig, roots, cane, vines, porcupine quills, feathers, and a variety of animal tissues, either plaited or used in an untwisted state. The articles produced were mats, blankets, nets, bags, plain cloths, hats, belts, and sandals.

It is probable that in many instances a simple frame was used for weaving. The threads of the warp were fixed and the woof was passed back and forth between them, but the form of fabric in which the threads are twisted in pairs at each crossing of the woof could have been made only by hand.

Adair tells us that formerly the Indians made very handsome carpets. "They have a wild hemp that grows about six feet high, in open, rich, level lands, and which usually ripens in July: it is plenty on our frontier settlements. When it is fit for use, they pull, steep, peel, and beat it; and the old women spin it off the distaffs, with wooden machines, having some clay on the middle of them, to hasten the motion. When the coarse thread is prepared, they put it into a frame about six feet square, and instead of a shuttle, they thrust through the thread with a long cane, having a large string through the web, which they shift at every second course of the thread. When they have thus finished their arduous labour, they paint each side of the carpet with such figures, of various colors, as their fruitful imaginations devise; particularly the images of those birds and beasts they are acquainted with; and likewise of themselves, acting in their social stations. There is that due proportion, and so much wild variety in the design, that would really strike a curious eye with pleasure and admiration.

"The women are the chief,if not the only manufacturers; the men judge that if they performed this office, it would exceedingly depreciate them. In the winter season, the women gather buffalo's hair, a sort of coarse brown curled wool; and having spun it as fine as they can, and properly doubled it, they put small beads of different colours upon the yarn, as they work it: the figures they work in those small webs, are generally uniform, but sometimes they diversify them on both sides."

In early times porcupine quills were employed in the ornamentation of Cherokee pipes, mocasins, and articles of clothing. Swanson writes, "For this purpose they take off the quills of the porcupine which are white and black. They split them fine enough to use in embroidery. They dye a part of the white red, another part yellow, while a third part remains white. Ordinarily they embroider on black skin, and then they dye the black a redish brown. But if they embroider on the tree bark the black always remains the same.

"Their designs are rather similar to some of those which one finds in Gothic architecture. They are composed of straight lines which form right angles where they meet, which a common person would call the corner of a square. They also make designs of the same style on the mantles and coverings which they fashion out of mulberry bark."

Spinning wheels and looms were first used shortly before the American Revolution, being brought in by an Englishman in 1770 who taught their use to his Cherokee wife.

Cherokee girl demonstrates her skill in weaving with a four harness loom.

Pottery fragments with impressions of woven materials. From an early Cherokee village site at Tuckaseegee, North Carolina. From the collection of Dwight Moses.

Bird knotting and plain tapestry weaving by Cindy Taylor. This type of loom is thought to have been used by the ancient Cherokee. Courtesy Indian Arts and Crafts Board.

The art of spinning and weaving in the Cherokee villages was expanded when missionaries established the first schools in the Indian territory. Cherokee women continued the practice until machine woven goods became plentiful and easy to obtain. It was the practice for certain women of the tribe to make their living by weaving cloth from which other members of the tribe made clothing. During the earlier part of this century, weaving became almost an art of the past for the Cherokee, though it never entirely disappeared.

There has been a revival of hand weaving on the Reservation in recent years, and it has grown steadily in popularity. A number of Cherokee women have looms in their homes and add greatly to the family income by weaving in their spare time. Numerous materials including wool, cotton, linen, corn shucks, wood strips, rush, cane, broom-sedge, and other native materials are used in their woven projects. Afghans, blankets, and scarves of wool, and runners, luncheon sets, and towels of linen are among the most popular hand woven articles produced.

Native dyes are used almost exclusively. Broom-sedge, apple bark, marigolds, bloodroot (called paccoonroot by the Indians), dahlias, or almost any grass or weed produces shades of yellow. For the browns and tans, walnut bark, roots, leaves and hulls are used. For rose-tan, hemlock, and for the apricot shade, touch-me-nots are used. Red and rose come from madder. Indigo is used for the blues, and shades of gray are obtained from black wool.

Only Indian patterns are used by the Cherokee weavers. Some of these patterns are traditional, some are adapted from basket designs, and some are the creations of present day weavers. One of the most popular patterns is the "Road to Soco" design created by Roxana Stamper. Roxana lives on Soco Mountain and her design represents the zigzag trail that leads up the valley past towering peaks of the Smokies to her home. Some of the other patterns created, named, and used by the Cherokee are: flying geese, running water, bear's paw, squash blossom, snow flake, and sacred bird.

The "Road-to-Soco" design created by Roxana Standingdeer is shown here on a large cross-stitched wall hanging. The design represents the winding trails and peaks up Soco Mountain.

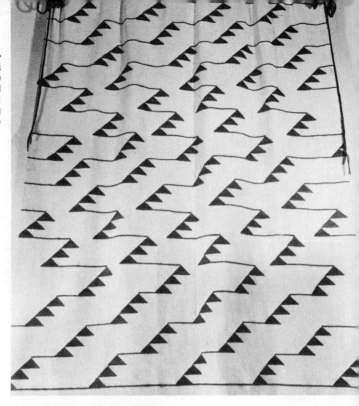

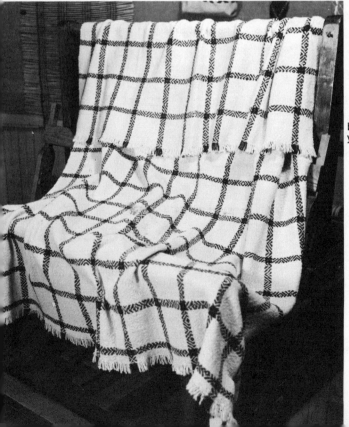

Hand-woven Cherokee blanket of vegetable-dyed yarn.

Loom woven scarf by a Cherokee crafts-man. Courtesy Indian Arts and Crafts Board.

Neck scarf. Loom woven of wool yarn by Roxie Stamper. Courtesy Indian Arts and Crafts Board.

Cherokee textiles. The blanket is hand woven of vegetable-dyed wool. The skirts are hand woven of wool and cotton. The handbag has a cross-stitched design on monks cloth. The design on the bag has been adapted from an old Cherokee basket design.

Cloth dolls of an Indian boy and girl.

Cherokee cloth dolls by Caroline Sneed. Notice the tiny basket the woman is carrying and the baby strapped to her back, both features typical of the Cherokee. The floor and back of picture show hand-woven mats of native material.

In addition to loom woven projects, the Cherokee are quite skilled at finger weaving. Scarves, sashes, belts and other objects from two to eight inches wide are made by this technique. Dyed wool yarn is used and a skilled weaver is able to manipulate 200 or more strands at one time. The more strands used the wider the object. Both a single and double weave method are used. Weaving is accomplished by anchoring all the strands at one end and then braiding them diagonally back and forth across the item. An unlimited variety of patterns is possible and great skill is required. The Cherokee have revived this art of their ancestors and are believed to be the only Indians of the United States practicing it today.

Three Cherokee women producing beautiful articles by the finger weaving technique are Mary Lossiah Shell, Helen Bradley Smith and Nancy Littlejohn. Some of the loom weavers are Lula O. Gloyn, Cecelia Taylor, Roxana Stamper, Amanda Walker, Pearl Saunooke, Bessie Wildcat and Maggie Ben.

STONECRAFTS

The early Cherokee used many utilitarian objects made of stone. Some of these were bowls, chisels, gouges, adzes, axes, spades, hoes, knives, drills, scrapers, celts (used in skinning animals), mortars and pestles. Both bell-shaped and roller pestles were used. The stone mortars and pestles were later abandoned in favor of wooden ones for grinding corn.

Stone weapons included war clubs made with a round stone, spearpoints and arrowheads. Both flint and quartzite were used for the last two. Quartzite was more difficult to work and chip than flint, and arrowheads and spearpoints of this material were generally not as well shaped as those made from flint.

"Chunkey" or discoidal stones, used to play the game of "chunkey", represent some of the finest craftsmanship of the Woodland Indians. These stone disks, five to six inches in diameter an dbout two inches thick, had concave sides and were sometimes pierced. They were made from quartzite, granite or other soft-grained stone, were almost perfectly symmetrical and were highly polished. The game of "chunkey" was played with these disks on a large smooth clay court by two persons at a time. The stone was rolled down the center of the court by one player, then both players hurled a pointed wooden spear after the rolling stone. The player whose spear stopped nearest the stone at the time it came to rest won the contest. These chunky or discoidal stones were regarded as the property of the town.

The Cherokee also used stone objects for ornamental, ceremonial and religious purposes. Some of these were beads, charms, gorgets, bannerstones, boatstones and birdstones. The position in which some stone gorgets are found

Cherokee brave using a flint-tipped shaft to drill pipestone. Finished pipes are shown on bench. Oconaluftee Indian Village. Courtesy Cherokee Historical Association.

Effigy pipes of stone and a clay pipe (left). The Cherokee were widely known for their skill in pipe making. They often traded pipes for copper, shell and other materials not native to their region. Museum of the Cherokee Indian, Cherokee, North Carolina.

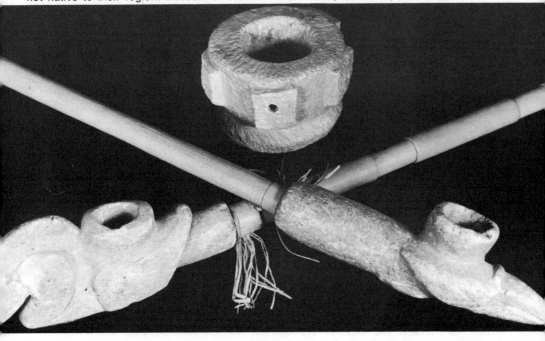

Cherokee peace pipes. The peace pipe was large, plain or effigial, and had one or more stem holes. The round pipe has five stem holes and is six inches in diameter. In all cases smoking among primitive Indians was a ritual, not a habit. Museum of the Cherokee Indians, Cherokee, North Carolina.

Individual Cherokee pipes were small, sometimes with stem complete, more often fitted with cane or wooden stems. The wooden stems pictured are recent additions. The initiation pipe in the center is a rare type of great interest. When a chief was inducting another into office, both of them took a puff from this double-bowl pipe—which may have had a divided stem—and thus pledged their joint allegiance to the tribe and its laws. Museum of the Cherokee Indian, Cherokee, North Carolina.

Cherokee stone objects. The large axe was made by fitting the head into a slit in a limb of a cedar tree and allowing the limb to grow. This secured the stone so firmly it could not be moved. The handle was then cut and shaped, bound with sinew, rattlesnake skin, and buckskin. This specimen was found in a deep dry cave and owes its preservation to its not having been buried. Center left is a one-piece ceremonial hatchet (Kirksey collection). Center right a celt for skinning animals. Lower right a wild-turkey hunter's call. The use of piece shown at lower left is unknown. Museum of the Cherokee Indian, Cherokee, North Carolina.

In graves suggests that they were worn as ornaments on the chest. Many show engraved designs, suggesting that they had some symbolic meaning to their owners. Boatstones are thought to have been used as talismans or charms by the Woodland Indians, possibly to insure against disasters when traveling in canoes. Bannerstones were probably mounted on the ends of decorated rods and used as symbols or insignia of authority. The forms are numerous, and each stone may represent only a portion of a banner which was made of wood and other materials that have long since disintergrated. Birdstones may have been used by medicine men. One early traveler has left a record of the fact that some medicine men wore a small black bird over one ear as a badge of office.

In pipes more than in anything else, the early Cherokee seem to have shown individuality. Both earthenware and stone were used and at Nacoochee the pipe-making industry seems to have reached a high state of development. The area of eastern Tennessee, western North Carolina, and northern Georgia seems to have been the center of pipe smokers and here a large number of pipe types were created. It is believed that pipes from this area were used as an item of trade with other tribes for such things as copper from the Great Lakes area and shells from the coast. Mica from Virginia and North Carolina was also spread by trade through much of the mound building area. The stone pipes, which varied greatly in size, were usually made of pipestone, a greenish steatite, which was soft enough to carve easily with flint knives and take a high polish. Many large, heavy stone pipes carved in the effigies of men, birds and animals, have been found in the states south of the Ohio River. These effigies were the largest of all Indian pipes and sometimes reached the length of eighteen inches, a height of ten inches and weight of eighteen pounds. As a general rule the more remarkable of them may be regarded as the public property of the tribe.

Adair reports, "They make beautiful stone pipes and the Cherokee the best of any of the Indians for their mountainous country contains many different sorts and colours of soils

Stone mortar and bell pestle used by the early Cherokee for grinding corn. This mortar was found on the reservation while excavation was under way for the Mountainside Theatre. Stone mortars were later abandoned in favor of wooden ones. The Indian discovered that the grit from the stone was wearing off his teeth.

Cherokee discoidal stones represent very skilled craftsmanship. They were made of many kinds of stone and were almost always found in matching pairs. Dark center discoidal is five inches in diameter. They were used in the game of "chunkey". Museum of the Cherokee Indian, Cherokee, North Carolina.

John J. Wilnoty, outstanding primitive sculptor, carving stone pipes. Courtesy Cherokee Historical Association.

Recent stone sculpture. Carved from native pipestone by John J. Wilnoty.

proper for such uses. They easily form them with their toma-
hawks, and afterward finish them in any desired form with
their knives; the pipes being of a very soft quality till they are
smoked with, and use to the fire, when they become quite
hard. They are often a full span long, and the bowls are
about half as large again as those of our English pipes. The
fore part of each commonly runs out with a sharp peak, two
or three fingers broad, and a quarter of an inch thick—on
both sides of the bowl, lengthwise, they cut several pictures
with a great deal of skill and labour; such as a buffalo and
a panther on the opposite sides of the bowl; a rabbit and a
fox; and, very often, a man and a woman *puris naturalibus.*
Their sculpture cannot much be commended for its modesty.
The natives work so slow that one of their artists is two
months at a pipe with his knife before he finishes it; indeed,
as before observed, they are great enemies to profuse sweat-
ing, and are never in a hurry about a good thing. The stems
are commonly made of soft wood about two feet long, and
an inch thick, cut into four squares, each scooped till they
join very near the hollow of the stem; the beaus always hollow the squares, except a little at each corner to hold them
together, to which they fasten a parcel of bell-buttons, different sorts of fine feathers, and several small battered pieces
of copper kettles hammered, round deer-skin thongs, and a
red painted scalp; this is a boasting, valuable, and superlative
ornament. According to their standard, such a pipe constitutes the possessor, a grand beau. They so accurately carve,
or paint hieroglyphic characters on the stem, that the war-
actions, and the tribe of the owner, with a great many circumstances of things, are fully delineated."

A very limited amount of work in stone is being done by
the present day Cherokee. Spearpoint and arrowhead chipping is demonstrated to the public in Oconaluftee Indian Village. The demonstrator breaks the flint to approximate size
and then roughs the point to shape by tapping it with a river
stone. The final chipped edge is achieved by pressing it with
a piece of deer antler.

One Cherokee man, John J. Wilnoty, has revived the art

of stone carving. He makes pipes, gorgets, bowls and sculptured items. His sculptures are in great demand and many of his items have become museum pieces. Mr. Wilnoty is also a skilled wood carver and his wild cherry sculpture of an eagle dancer is described in the chapter on woodcrafts.

BEADS AND SHELL

The early Cherokee, like other Indian tribes, were great admirers of ornaments and used shell, bone, animal teeth, stone and metal to make necklaces, collars, bracelets, ear pins and gorgets. Shell was obtained from the coast and copper from the Great Lakes area through trade.

Turtle and turkey bones were used in necklaces. Bears' teeth were spaced between other beads in both bracelets and necklaces. Bone was also used for needles, fish hooks, awls and hair pins. Turtle shells and gourds were used to make rattles. Several turtle shell rattles filled with small pebbles were often strapped to the lower legs of women when they performed native dances.

The white shell gorgets or breast oranments found in Tennessee and neighboring states rank high among our best examples of aboriginal art. These shell discs, often six or seven inches in diameter, cut from large marine univalve shells have been frequently found in graves of both sexes in a position to indicate that they had been worn from the neck. Upon these shell gorgets the aboriginal artist skillfully pierced or engraved well proportioned designs which were often paragons of symmetry. These depict fighting and dancing human figures in elaborate ceremonial regalia, zoomorphic representations of the rattlesnake, spider, and turkey and various geometric motifs.

Reports indicate that during early historic times the Cherokee continued work in shell similar to that found in the mounds of their prehistoric ancestors. Lawson, who traveled through North Carolina in 1700, states that "The Indians oftentimes make of a certain large seashell a sort of gorget, which they wear about their neck on a string, so it hangs on

Cherokee bead-workers using imported Venetian beads. Oconaluftee Indian Village. Courtesy Cherokee Historical Association.

Cherokee beadwork is bright and colorful. Bracelets, necklaces, belts, and lapel pins are made chiefly for the tourist trade. Designs used are not always of Cherokee origin.

Cherokee beadwork. Photographed at 1968 Cherokee Indian Fair.

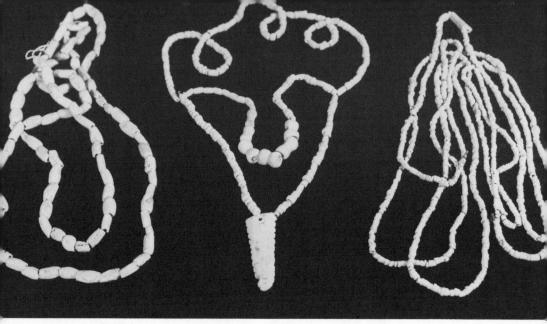

Early Cherokee shell beads. As many as fifteen thousand have been found in a single grave. Museum of the Cherokee Indian, Cherokee, North Carolina.

Shell gorgets and death mask. Shell gorgets perhaps had some ceremonial purpose. Some of them are perforated for wearing on the breast in bead necklaces. The ying yang and swastika emblems were often used on gorgets. The death mask has crude markings for eyes, nose and mouth. Mask was placed over the face of the corpse when buried. Museum of the Cherokee Indian, Cherokee, North Carolina.

Necklaces of corn beads and pony beads. Photographed at 1968 Cherokee Indian Fair.

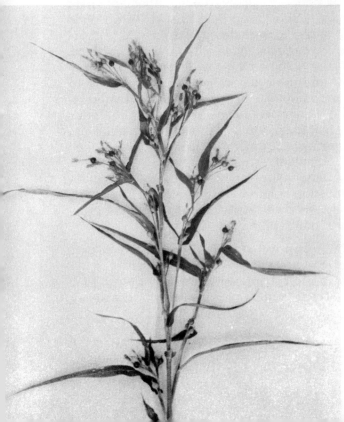

Bead corn stalk. The dark seed are mature and ready for harvesting.

their collar, whereon is sometimes engraven a cross or some odd sort of figure which comes, next to their fancy." Beverly, in his *History of Virginia*, evidently alluding to the same custom, says, "of this shell (the conch) they also make round tablets of about four inches in diameter which they polish as smooth as the other and sometimes they etch or engrave thereon circles, stars, a half-moon, or any other figure suitable to their fancy." Adair states, in his *History of the American Indians*, that "the priest wears a breast plate made of a conch shell with two holes bored in the middle." Adair also states, "Both the men and women who could afford it adorned themselves with great quantities of beads of various sizes and colours; sometimes wrought in garters,sashes, necklaces, and in strings round their wrists; and so from the crown of their heads sometimes to the cartilage of the nose. And they dote on them so much as to make them their current money in all payments to this day.

"Before we supplied them with our European beads, they had great quantities of wampum; (the Buccimum of the ancients) made out of conch-shell, by rubbing them on hard stones, and they form them according to their liking. With these they bought and sold at a stated current rate, without the least variation for circumstances either of time or place; and now they will hear nothing patiently of loss or gain, or allow us to heighten the price of our goods, be our reasons ever so strong, or though the exigencies and changes of time may require it. Formerly, four deer skins was the price of a large conch-shell bead, about the length and thickness of a man's forefinger; which they fixed to the crown of their head, as a high ornament—so greatly they valued them. Their beads bear a very near resemblance to ivory." As many as fifteen thousand shell beads have been found in a single grave and with only the crude tools available it would probably require several hours to make a single bead.

Present day Cherokee women have revived the ancient and colorful art of beadwork. Some of it is woven on small looms, but the most popular articles are made with the fingers and a needle. These include necklaces of various styles, belts, buttons, ear rings, and lapel ornaments. They use three sizes of brightly colored imported Venetian beads just as their ancestors did 200 years ago. The two smaller sizes are called seed beads and the larger size is known as pony beads. Usually only one size bead is used in an individual article.

Bead corn, sometimes known as Jacob's tears, is also used by the present day Cherokee in their beadwork. This plant is not native to the Cherokee area, but was imported from the Orient where several varieties are known. The stalks of this grain grow from two to six feet tall and the beads (seed) are formed on the tassels rather than in ears. The beads do not all mature at the same time and are harvested when they change from white to shades of grey, lavender or black. A small tassel protrudes from the end of each bead which is easily pulled out making a convenient and proper size hole for stringing. The beads are about the size of small marbles and when dry are almost as hard as stone. They have a high luster resembling pearls and no protective finish or polishing is needed. Some Indian mothers use a string of these beads instead of a teething ring for their infants. When strung into necklaces and bracelets, several brightly colored pony beads are usually added between each corn bead.

Dora Owle Palmer and Jane Youngdeer are among the Cherokee women producing attractive articles with seed and pony beads. Lula N. Welch is recognized for her creative use of bead corn.

Turtle shell and gourd rattles being used in native dance. Several turtle shell rattles are strapped to the lower leg of the Cherokee woman dancer. Oconaluftee Indian Village. Courtesy Cherokee Historical Association.

METALCRAFTS

It is a fact well established by years of painstaking field-work and research into old Spanish documents, that as metallurgists, the aboriginal inhabitants of North and South America ranked high among the prehistoric people of the world.

Before Columbus ever sailed, the Red Men knew and used tin, gold, silver, copper, mercury, lead, platinum, and even meteoric iron. Not only were the North American coppersmiths skilled in making weapons and ornaments from copper nugget, but also they displayed remarkable skill in beating out large, thin plates of the red metal and embossing beautiful designs on them. This embossing or repoussé work was done with a sharp bone or an antler point, the copper sheet being placed on some yielding surface such as a piece of buckskin laid on sand. One example of such ornamentation, found in a mound in Georgia, is the representation of an elaborately costumed winged god which closely resembles one of the Aztec deities. Other evidence of Mexican influence has been found in stone and shell work of the area. The better quality copper nugget seems to have come from the Great Lakes area, being obtained through trade.

In pre-Columbian times the Cherokee Indians, in what is now Georgia, are reported to have discovered gold and worked the precious metal into ornaments. They recovered this gold by panning and also by lode mining and did extensive prospecting in the gold district of north Georgia.

In historic times the use of silver replaced that of copper almost completely for ornaments. Practically all silver was from the coins of European and American countries. Silver

Copper bowl, iron candle holders and maple plate. This round, pleated copper bowl is a favorite with tourists and is made in several sizes by the Cherokee.

Metal breast plates and helmets to be worn by De Soto's men in the drama "Unto These Hills" were constructed in the Cherokee School metal shop.

was worked by most of the Southeastern tribes as well as the Cherokee.

Men, and sometimes women, worked in silver, using little hammers, anvils, vises, and other tools, obtained from the whites. They pounded out coins into round, flat, or oval pieces, cut them into smaller parts or drew them out into wires. According to the ornament desired, they selected a silver quarter, or a fifty cent piece, or a Mexican dollar, laid it on the side of an axe, and beat it a little with a hammer. Then they took it up with a pair of pliers, held it in the fire until it was almost red hot, and dipped it in water so as to cool it a little, after which they again pounded it. The heating was to prevent it from cracking. This process was gone through with several times, considerable force being used at first which was afterward moderated as the metal got thinner so as to make it smooth. Ornamental holes and indentations were made with an awl, and a larger hole was pierced in the middle with the same implement, its size being still further increased by means of a small knife. At the side of this aperture a small hole was punched with the awl, a common brass pin inserted in this, and bent over at the end so that it would not come out. When the ornament was to be fastened upon the dress, it was laid against the place to which it was to be attached, convex side out. Some of the cloth was then pulled through the central opening, the pin was run through the cloth, and when the fabric was pulled back, the ornament was held firm in place. Pieces intended for earrings were hammered down flat, after which a portion of one edge was cut off straight, a small hole punched in the middle of this straight side, and an iron or copper wire run through it and fastened to the ear. Silver braclets, rings, gorgets, spangles, and hair ornaments were also made.

Only a limited amount of work in metal is being done by the present day Cherokee. One attractive item which they make for sale in the craft shops is a round, hammered, copper bowl. This is made from flat sheets of copper and is raised to shape by repeated annealing and hammering. The tops of these bowls are tapered in by making folds or pleats in the metal.

They also make a small amount of sterling silver jewelry which is similar to the silver work now being done by the Southwestern Indians of the United States.

Another interesting metalsmith activity performed recently by the Cherokee was the construction of suits of armor to be worn by actors, representing De Soto's soldiers in the drama, Unto These Hills.

WEAPON MAKING

Blowguns were used by several Southeastern Indian tribes, but those of the Cherokee were outstanding for their workmanship and accuracy. They were capable of being blown with considerable force and would kill small game and birds. Perfectly straight river canes eight to ten feet long were hollowed out with a flint point reamer which was made by attaching the flint to the end of a smaller cane. Some skilled blowgun makers would rifle the inside of the cane barrel with spiral grooves for added accuracy.

Blowgun darts were made of slender shafts of locust wood and were tufted with thistledown from the bull thistle. The down is tied on one end of the shaft for a length of several inches and the other end of the dart is sharpened. Blowgun and dart construction and use are demonstrated for the public at Oconaluftee Indian Village in Cherokee.

Any doubt that bows and arrows have been used by the American Indians for thousands of years was dispelled in 1956. T. M. N. Lewis writes: "The discovery of a section of a two-thousand-year-old arrowshaft in a site in Green County, Tennessee, settled the question. Althought only eight and a half inches long, the cane arrowshaft section was the nock end. The cane, known as 'switch cane', is a slender, tough variety that grows in uplands. It was used for arrowshafts by the historic Cherokee who called it *guni* (goon'ee) the same word that they used for 'arrow'. The nock in the prehistoric example was made just beyond a joint; this prevented the shaft from splitting when the bow string was drawn taut. By fortunate accident, the short section of cane had been charred in some ancient fire. This accounted for its preservation, for wood that has been carbonized resists decay. Lying undisturbed five feet below the surface of the ground for more than twenty centuries, this unprepossessing fragment of char-coal became an important archaeological clue when it was carefully unearthed in 1956 by an amateur archaeologist. It proved beyond doubt that the early Woodland Indians used the bow and arrow." Most Cherokee arrowheads were of the triangular shape and these were fastened to the cane arrowshaft with bear gut. Feathers were placed on the shaft in a position that caused the arrow to spiral while in flight.

Bows of the Cherokee are generally made of locust wood, although the osage or mock orange is also recognized as a good bowwood because of its strength and resiliency. Bow-wood was often an item of trade among early Indians. Bows are usually five to six feet long, were carved with a flint knife and strung with deer sinew. The bow and arrow was consi-dered the chief weapon of the Indians before the white man brought guns.

Lanman, writing in 1848, told of a Cherokee blacksmith named Salola, or the Squirrel, whose hand-made rifles and pistols were the wonder of his contemporaries. He is believed to be the first Indian who ever manufactured an entire gun. In addition to fire-arms, he made grist mills and supplied the whole of Qualla Town with axes and ploughs.

Cherokee blowgun maker reaming out length of river cane. A metal reamer is being used in this photograph, but earlier Cherokee used a flint point attached to a length of cane as a reaming tool. Oconaluftee Indian Village. Courtesy Cherokee Historical Association.

Cherokee man making darts for blowgun. Bull thistle down is tied to sharpened locust shafts. Oconaluftee Indian Village. Courtesy Cherokee Historical Association.

Cherokee man using flint knife to carve a bow. Oconaluftee Indian Village. Courtesy Cherokee Historical Association.

Cherokee man using deer antler to chip flint arrowheads and spear points. He is wearing a bear tooth necklace. Oconaluftee Indian Village. Courtesy Cherokee Historical Association.

Bird points, notched spears, singing arrows and stone drills. Bird points are the small-
est of all arrow heads. The notched spears (top center) show perfection of workmanship.
Singing arrows (right) were tipped with beveled, serrated flints that made them spin and
sing in flight. Museum of the Cherokee Indian, Cherokee, North Carolina.

FEATHERS

Feathers were used by the Cherokee in many ways. The headdress is probably the best known feathered item used by Indians. The early Cherokee usually used only one, two or three feathers of the wildturkey, eagle or hawk as a hair ornament and were never known to use the bulky, gaudy headdresses often displayed today at Indian tourist attractions. The chief would wear a more elaborate headdress at council meetings and ceremonial occasions. This was ornamented with swan, white crane or other exotic feathers from coastal birds often obtained through trade.

Clothing made of feathers was worn by both men and women. Such items as skirts, mantels and robes were fashioned from the breastfeathers of the wild turkey. Bark was used with the feathers to make strips which were then assembled so that the feathers overlapped as on the body of a bird. Brightly colored feathers from the cardinal, bluebird or other native birds were worked into these garments making them very attractive. These articles were very practical, since they were both light weight and warm.

Feathers were used for other purposes such as feathering arrows, constructing fans and making wands used in the Cherokee Eagle Dance. A quill was sometimes used to scribe designs on pottery.

Little use is made of feathers by the present day Cherokee. Some few are used to decorate items made for the tourist trade.

Tail feathers of the wild turkey were used to make this cloak. Oconaluftee Indian Village. Courtesy Cherokee Historical Association.

Mantle made from the breast feathers of the wild turkey. Headdress is type worn by chiefs at council meetings. Oconaluftee Indian Village. Courtesy Cherokee Historical Association.

LEATHERCRAFTS

The Cherokee, as did all American Indian tribes, made extensive use of animal hides in their everyday life. De Soto's journalists in 1540 described the fine robes of skin worn by the Cherokee and mentioned a dressed buffalo skin given the expedition.

The technique employed by early Indians to tan and process hides is described by T. M. N. Lewis as follows:

The processing of hides and the fashioning of them into clothing, footwear, bedding, containers, straps and thongs formed a major industry, probably engaged in by women exclusively and almost continuously. It is a craft,already ancient in the days of the Archaic Indians, whose modern practice grew out of painstaking, trial-and-error experiments of forgotten peoples. The common Indian method of preparing hides was to stretch the skin on the ground and scrape it clean, removing the flesh with bone or antler scrapers, and the hair with flint blades. The usual tanning was merely a matter of smearing the hide with the fat, brains and liver of the animal and then soaking it in water overnight. Sometimes, the skin was also smoked. Next, it was stretched on a pole framework to dry, and finally made pliable by working between the hands or sliding back and forth across a pole.

While flint knives were the cutting tools used in leather work, all of the assembling was done with bone awls and needles. The basic form of the needle, even to the elongated eye, invented in Paleolithic times in the Old World, has not changed today, except with respect to the material from which it is made. The large number

Braided horsehair bridle of great strength. The one pictured is over eighty years old and is a beautiful example of delicate braiding. Museum of the Cherokee Indian, Cherokee, North Carolina.

of bone awls found on Archaic Indian sites indicates that leather was very important in the daily life of the people.

Deerhide probably formed the most important single material used in native dress. It was also used for heads of drums and as the cover for the small balls used in the Indian ball games. Bear skins were used for heavy winter robes and bed coverings, as were bison hides before they disappeared from the southeastern part of the United States. Moccasins were also cut from bear skins. Both sexes of the Cherokee wore moccasins that were made like short boots and reached half way up the leg.

The Cherokee were good saddlers and bridle makers. Adair says, "they can finish a saddle with their usual instruments, without any kind of iron to bind the work: but the shape of it is so antiquated and mean, and so much like those of the Dutch West-Indians, that a person would be led to imagine they had formerly met, and been taught the art in the same school. The Indians provide themselves with a quantity of white oak boards, and notch them, so as to fit the saddle-trees; which consist of two pieces before, and two behind, crossing each other in notches, about three inches below the top ends of the frame. Then they take a buffalo green hide, covered with its winter curls, and having properly shaped it to the frame, they sew it with large thongs of the same skin, as tight and secure as need be; when it is thoroughly dried, it appears to have all the properties of a cuirass saddle. A trimmed bear-skin serves for a pad; and formerly, their bridle was only a rope around the horse's neck, with which they guided him at pleasure."

A bridle made by the Cherokee prior to 1880 is on display at the Museum of the Cherokee Indian on the Qualla Reservation in Western North Carolina. The bridle is artistic and well made and is practically one hundred percent horse hair. It was platted in such a fashion as to give it great strength and durability. There are also in the museum specimens of fish lines that were platted from several strands of horses tail.

BIBLIOGRAPHY

Adair, James, *History of the American Indians*, London, 1775.

Alexander, H., "Art of the American Indian", *Nation*, May 6, 1931.

Appleton, LeRoy H., *Indian Art of the Americas*, Charles Scribners Sons, New York, 1950.

Armstrong, Zella, *History of Hamilton County and Chattanooga, Tennessee*, Vol. I, Lookout Publishing Company, Chattanooga, 1931.

"Artists with Never a Thought for Fame", *Literary Digest,* September 9, 1933.

"Arts, Crafts Exhibits Scheduled at Cherokee", *Asheville Citizen-Times*, February 18, 1951.

Bartram, William, *Travels*, Philadelphia, 1791.

Blanton, John O., *Prehistoric Man in Tennessee*, Tracy City News, Tracy City, Tennessee, 1896.

Blythe, Jarrett, "Paleface Visit Indian Band and Buy Trinkets", *Asheville Citizen-Times,* January 17, 1939.

"Bridle Made by Cherokee Indian", *Asheville Citizen-Times,* September 11, 1950.

Campbell, Robert F., "Cherokee Indians Open Fair", *Asheville Citizen,* October 4, 1950.

Catlin, George, *North American Indians*, Vol. II, Leary Stuart and Company, Philadelphia, 1913.

"Cherokee Indian Fair", Program for 1968.

"Cherokee Indian Fair Scheduled", *Asheville Citizen,* September 25, 1968.

"Cherokee Plan Puts Stress on Crafts", *Asheville Citizen-Times*, June 17, 1939.

Coe, Joffre L., "Archaeology of North Carolina", *Bulletin of the Archaeological Society of North Carolina*, May, 1937.

"Cooperative Handicraft Shop Opens at Cherokee", *Asheville Citizen-Times*, April 28, 1946.

Corley, Victor, "Cherokee Indians, Real Discoverers of Rocky Mountain Gold", *Hobbies*, May, 1942.

Crowninshield, F., D'Harnoncourt, R., "American Indian, Artist", *House and Garden*, June, 1934.

Culin, Stewart, "Games of the North American Indians", *Twenty-fourth Annual Report Bureau of American Ethnology*, Washington, 1902, 1903.

Dickinson, E. M., "A Nuisance Converted into a Blessing", *The Playground*, July, 1926, Vol. 20, p. 221-4.

Douglas, Frederic H., *Colors in Indian Arts,* Denver Art Museum leaflet 56, Denver, Colorado, 1933.

Indian Basketry, Denver Art Museum leaflet 58, Denver, Colorado, 1933.

Symbolism in Indian Art, Denver Art Museum leaflet 61, Denver, Colorado, 1934.

Design Areas in Indian Art, Denver Art Museum leaflet 62, Denver, Colorado, 1934.

Indian Vegetable Dyes, Part I, Denver Art Museum leaflet 63, Denver, Colorado, 1934.

Basketry Construction Technics, Denver Art Museum leaflet 67, Denver, Colorado, 1935.

Basketry Decoration Technics, Denver Art Museum leaflet 68, Denver, Colorado, 1935.

Indian Vegetable Dyes, Part II, Denver Art Museum leaflet 71, Denver, Colorado, 1936.

Indian Basketry East of the Rockies, Denver Art Museum leaflet 87, Denver, Colorado, 1939.

Douglas, Frederic H., and D'Harnoncourt, Rene, *Indian Art of the United States*, The Museum of Modern Art, New York, 1941.

Drake, Samuel G., *The Aboriginal Races of North America,* Hurst and Company, New York, 1880.

Dunn, D., "Indian Children Carry Forward Old Traditions", *School Arts Magazine*, March, 1935.

Eaton, Allen H., *Handicrafts of the Southern Highlands,* Russell Sage Foundation, New York, 1937.

Fundaburk, Emma Lila, and Foreman, Mary Douglass, *Sun Circles and Human Hands*, Published by the author, Luverne, Alabama, 1957.

Furry, Margaret S., and Viemont, Bess M., *Home Dyeing with Natural Dyes*, United States Government Printing Office, Washington, D. C., 1935.

Gilbert, William Harlen, Jr., "The Eastern Cherokees", *Bureau of American Ethnology*, Bulletin 133, Washington, 1943.

Harrington, R., *Cherokee and Earlier Remains on Upper Tennessee River*, Museum of the American Indian, Heye Foundation, New York, 1922.

Henderson, R., "American Indians' Contribution to Design", *House Beautiful*, April, 1930.

Heye, G. G., Hodge, F. W., and Pepper, G. H. *The Nacoochee Mound in Georgia*, Museum of the American Indian Heye Foundation, New York, 1918.

Holmes, W. H., "Aboriginal Pottery of the Eastern United States", *Twentieth Annual Report Bureau of American Ethnology*, Washington, 1903.
"Prehistoric Textile Art of Eastern United States", *Thirteenth Annual Report of Bureau of American Ethnology*, Washington, 1896.

"Honeysuckle Basketry Exhibit Honors Craftsman Lucy George", *Asheville Citizen-Times*, May 17, 1970.

Huxley, A., "American Sources of Modern Art", *New Republic*, May 31, 1933.

"Indian as an Artist", *Literary Digest*, December 26, 1931.

James, George Wharton, *Indian Basketry; Its Poetry and Symbolism*, National Education Association, 1903.
Indian Basketry and How to Make Baskets, Printed privately by the author, Pasadena, California, 1903.

Lanman, Charles, *Letters from the Allegheny Mountains*, George P. Putman, New York, 1849.

Lawson, John, *Lawson's History of North Carolina*, London, 1714, reprint Richmond, Va., 1937.

Leftwich, Rodney L., "Cherokee White Oak Basketry", *School Arts*, September, 1954.
"Making Honeysuckle Baskets", *School Arts*, February, 1956.
"Cane Basketry of the Cherokees", *School Arts*, February, 1957.

Lewis, T. M. N., *Annotations Pertaining to Prehistoric Research in Tennessee*, University of Tennessee Record, Vol. 40, No. 6, Knoxville, 1937.

Lewis, T. M. N., and Kneberg, Madeline, *Tribes That Slumber*, University of Tennessee Press, Knoxville, 1958.

Malone, Henry Thompson, *Cherokee of the Old South*, University of Georgia Press, Athens, 1956.

Martin, P. S., Quimby, G. I., and Collier, Donald, *Indians Before Columbus*, University of Chicago Press, Chicago, 1947.

Mason, Otis T., *Aboriginal American Basketry*, United States National Museum, Annual Reports, Washington, 1902.

McCoy, George W., "Wedgewood Used Western North Carolina Clay", *Asheville Citizen-Times*, August 13, 1950.

McGuire, J. D., "Pipes and Smoking Customs of the American Aborigines", *United States National Museum Annual Report*, Washington, 1899.

Mooney, James, "Myths of the Cherokee", *Nineteenth Annual Report Bureau of American Ethnology*, Washington, 1900.

"The Sacred Formulas of the Cherokees", *Bureau of American Ethnology Annual Report*, Washington, 1891.

Moorhead, Warren King, *Exploration of the Etowah Site in Georgia*, Yale University Press, New Haven, 1932.

"Move Made to Revive Lost Art of Pottery Making by Cherokees", *Asheville Citizen*, September 25, 1939.

"Museum of Cherokee Indian", *Charlotte Observer*, June 14, 1950.

"Out-of-State Visitors See Cherokee Exhibit", *Asheville Citizen-Times*, May 28, 1950.

Parris, John, *The Cherokee Story*, The Stephens Press, Asheville, 1950.

"Kentucky Cane Growers to Sign Treaty with Cherokees August 13", *Asheville Citizen-Times*, August 6, 1950.

"Rich Mountain Flora Supplies Materials for Variety of Dyes", *The New Cherokee Phoenix*, Cherokee, N. C., August 14, 1951.

"Wilnoty is Considered Fine Primitive Sculptor", *Asheville Citizen*, April 8, 1969.

"Hominy Canebrakes Opened to Cherokee Craftsmen", *Asheville Citizen-Times*, May 13, 1969.

"Double-Weave an Ancient Pattern", *Asheville Citizen-Times*, May 18, 1969.

"Records Indicate Nununyi Existed", *Asheville Citizen-Times*, June 5, 1969.

"Qualla Exhibit Honors Eva Wolfe", *Asheville Citizen-Times,* November 30, 1969.

Richmond, Stephen, "Demonstration Workshop Program for the Cherokee and Choctaw Reservations", *Smoke Signals,* United States Department of the Interior, Indian Arts and Crafts Board, Washington, Spring, 1965.

Sequerira, C., "Culture That Was America's Before the 'White Man' Came", *Christian Science Monitor Magazine,* January 13, 1940.

Setzler, Frank M. and Jennings, Jesse D., "Peachtree Mound and Village Site, Cherokee County, North Carolina", Bulletin No. 131, *Bureau of American Ethnology,* Washington, 1941.

Shetrone, Henry Clyde, *The Mound Builders*, D. Appleton, New York and London, 1930.

Speck, Frank G., *Decorative Art and Basketry of the Cherokee*, Bulletin of the Public Museum of the City of Milwaukee, 1920.

Speck, Frank G., and Broom, Leonard, *Cherokee Dance and Drama*, University of California Press, Berkley, 1951.

Starkey, Marion, *The Cherokee Nation*, Alfred A. Knopf, New York, 1946.

Starr, Emmett, *History of the Cherokee Indians*, Warden Company, Oklahoma City, 1921.

Swanton, John R., "The Indians of the Southeastern United States", *Bureau of American Ethnology*, Bulletin 137, Washington, 1946.

Thomas, Cyrus, *The Cherokee in Pre-Columbian Times*, N. D. C. Hodges, New York, 1890.

Thurston, Gates P., *Antiquities of Tennessee*, Robert Clark Company, Cincinnati, 1765.

Timberlake, Lieut. Henry, *The Memoirs of Lieut. Henry Timberlake*, London, 1765.

Valliant, G. C., "North American Indian Art", *Magazine of Art*, November, 1939.

Webb, William S., "Archaeological Survey of Norris Basin", Bulletin No. 118, *Bureau of American Ethnology*, Washington, 1938.

Weltfish, Gene, "Prehistoric North American Basketry, Techniques and Modern Distributions", American Anthropological Association, *American Anthropologist*, new series, Vol. 32, pp. 454-495, Menasha, Wisconsin, 1930.

West, George A., *Tobacco Pipes and Smoking Customs of the American Indians*, Milwaukee Public Museum Bulletin, Milwaukee, 1934.

White, Mary, *How to Make Baskets*, with a chapter on "What the Basket Means to the Indian", Doubleday Page and Company, New York, 1902.

Williams, Samuel C., *Early Travels in the Tennessee Country*, The Watauga Press, Johnson City, Tennessee, 1928.

Witthoft, John, *Stone Pipes of the Historic Cherokees,* University of North Carolina, Chapel Hill, 1949.

Wormington, H. Marie, *Ancient Man in North America*, Denver Museum of Natural History, Denver, 1957.

Send for Free Catalog of Books by . . .

CHEROKEE PUBLICATIONS
P.O. Box 256
Cherokee, N.C. 28719

American Indian Prayers & Poetry

The Story of the Cherokee People

Cherokee Legends

The Cherokees, Past and Present

American Indian Cooking and Herblore

American Indian Color Book

Cherokee Fun and Learn Book

Magic Lake

Please Don't Step On Me
(An Indian Ecology Book For Children)

Indian America
(A Geography of North American Indians)

Cherokee Alphabet Card (6x9)

Sequoyah Card (6x9)